The Wartime Memoirs of Robert E. Lee

By

Edward Aronoff (Ghost Writer)

Three Came Home Publishing Co.
Box 1253 Banner Elk, NC 28604

Library of Congress Cataloging in Publication Data
Main entry under title:

The Wartime Memoirs of Robert E. Lee

1. English language – nonfiction
I. Three Came Home Publishing Company.
II. Title: The Wartime Memoirs of Robert E. Lee

ISBN: 978-1-62209-772-2

Printed in the United States of America

Cover design by Donald Consolver

Other books by Edward Aronoff

BETRAYAL AT GETTYSBURG

THREE CAME HOME: VOL. I – LORENA

THREE CAME HOME: VOL. II – SAM

THREE CAME HOME: VOL. III – RUTHERFORD

TOXIC FOOD/HEALTHY FOOD

LAST CHANCE

THE PAGLIACCI AFFAIR

To order any book, contact:

edwardaronoff@yahoo.com
or write:
Three Came Home Publishing
Box 1253, Banner Elk, NC 28604

Table of Contents

General Robert E. Lee –
His middle name is audacity!

THE WARTIME MEMOIRS OF ROBERT E. LEE

By Edward Aronoff
(Ghost Writer)

The legend begins

Robert E. Lee was already, at the beginning of the Civil War, a puzzle, an enigma wrapped in a mystery. No less an observer than the famous Southern diarist, Mary Chestnut described him as, "cold, quiet and grand." But, what was behind that cool exterior?

He was always polite and extremely kind and so aloof in manner most people, like Mary Chestnut, thought of him as remote. But those who saw him in a moment of passion, like the time at Gettysburg when he greeted the long absent Jeb Stuart with a raised fist, a bright red neck and his head jerking in spasms, knew him differently. Those who had seen the general in a ferocious fury like that knew to quickly beat a silent retreat.

When in June 1862 General Joe Johnston was wounded by the "shot heard 'round the Americas," and Lee took his place, the Federal General in command, George McClellan said, "I prefer Lee to Johnston, he is too weak... and wanting in moral firmness." BIG mistake, General McClellan!

But McClellan was not mistaken alone. Other men and even Southern newspapers were also being derogatory calling General Lee, *Evacuating Lee, Granny Lee,* and even the *King of Spades* (called so for insisting his men dig trenches for defense.)

One North Carolina newspaperman gave voice to a common belief about Lee in the South: "I do not like him, he 'falls back' too much... His nickname last summer was 'old-stick-in-the-mud'... There is already enough mud in and about our lines, and I pray God Lee will not fulfill the whole of his nick-name."

Nevertheless there were men who knew Lee better. One day, after the wounding of General Johnston, Colonel Joe Ives was asked by Major Porter Alexander, “Here we are Colonel Ives, digging and fortifying trenches for the King of Spades while McClellan and his bluebellies have all the time in the world to consolidate their forces and when they’re ready come at us like a herd of crazed bulls. Has General Lee the courage required for our scanty force to meet the enemies superior force…”

“Alexander!” Ives interrupted, “If there is one man in either army, head and shoulders above any other in daring it is General Lee! By God, his middle name is *Audacity*!

Finally the wounded General Joseph Johnston himself struck a blow for Lee when he answered a friend who said that Johnson’s wound could spell disaster for the Confederate cause. Johnston answered hotly. “No, Sir!” the general exclaimed, “the shot that struck me down is the very best for the Southern cause. He (General Lee) will do what I could never have done and that is to deal with the Southern Congress *and* concentrate our forces for the defense of the South.”

Robert E. Lee
Office of the President
Washington University
Lexington, Virginia

February 10, 1869

Smith Lee
Dept. of the Navy
Washington, D.C.

My dear Smith:

As you probably know, I have been prevailed upon by Harper's Weekly to Contribute my thoughts on the late unpleasantness in the form of a personal memoir.

When I was asked to do this project I thought, so many memoirs are being presented nowadays I hesitate to respond in the affirmative to the publisher. But, Harpers is insistent and they have assured me that it will not only be my pleasure but my duty to share my experiences with my fellow Southerners, and indeed with the world. So I acquiesced.

My approach will be as follows, each important incident and battle shall be written up by me as I saw it. But before I write any of it I shall endeavor to contact my own officers, and their Federal counterparts, and have them also give their observations on the battle in question. That will make for more even-handedness, don't you think?

As for my personal life I will keep that to a minimum, but I will revel in telling of my families' incidents of exemplary courage, loyalty and honor to their convictions. As you assuredly know my duties as an engineer and General for the Confederate Army led me far afield of Arlington and my family so they, and you too, dear brother, will have to help me fill in the gaps.

I will begin the memoirs with my happy years at Stratford Hall before our father was forced to leave us, and our dear mother, rest her soul, led us all forward supplying all of our needs on her pitiful pension. And I leave it to you dear brother to honor me by helping me, as a close observer, to help me write the first chapter.

Please give my best regards to your dear wife and children.

Your loving brother and obedient servant,

R.E.Lee

Preface

Sept. 20, 1870: Washington University

I have been urged so often by my family, students, friends and fellow officers to write my memoirs that I have finally consented to do so. (Also I now have a ghostwriter who will help me.)

Although I have written to newspapers, friends and colleagues, to help them answer an attack on them, or give an explanation of a battle plan, I have never given a comprehensive account of my actions and feelings during the late, War of Secession.

After Harper's Weekly contacted me and proposed that they shepherd me through the actual production without changing my beliefs, I thought it was time to lay aside what people supposed had happened and tell what really happened to me and my men. Ah, yes, my men.

Let me tell you what I think of the men of my army. They shall go on eternally, wrapped in gold and glory, those men who served with me in the Army of Northern Virginia.

In preparing my memoir I chastised myself never to do an injustice to anyone, North or South, and to limit myself to what I know and what I saw. If anyone else, Confederate or Union saw it differently, well, they have their opinion, for what it's worth.

Naturally a book of three or four hundred pages cannot fully tell everything that happened to our army, the subject is simply too vast. One must look to the individual commanders for the battle details and to the bravery of the individual Confederate soldiers who shed their blood and broke their hearts for, *The Cause.*

Before I hasten to tell my story I want to leave you, the reader, with one thought. I am eternally indebted to my children who, with their filial devotion, helped me to contact all those people who, with their truth, share with me the telling of my reminiscences of the Army of Northern Virginia in the American Civil War.

Your Obedient Servant,

R.E.Lee

P. S. I love these young men that Washington College is training to be good citizens and I must admit, because of my health, it is hard for me to continue on as president. Sadly, I have a premonition my end is near. But for the sake of Virginia, for the time being, I feel I must go on. Yes I love Virginia, and if I did not have such a love for my native state I would not have gone to war on the Confederate side.

****

Here it is already, October 1, 1870. Tempest fugit.

I write rapidly but the vertigo that plagues me is more frequent now. The chest pains I suffer are harder and longer each time they come and now sometimes even radiate up to my chin and down my left arm.

Like General Grant, who was my enemy and later my friend, I must hurry and complete this work before I… before I join all those who went before me.

And if I do go before this manuscript is done I want to wish my Virginia, my South, my Native Land, *goodnight*.

Prodigious birth of love

Shakespeare

Chapter 1: Birth and Boyhood

I was born in Stratford, Virginia with a silver spoon in my mouth. The reason it was silver was because of my sainted Mother, Ann Carter. The reason the silver soon turned to brass was because of my Father, Light Horse Harry Lee.

I am the fourth child born to Colonel Harry Lee and Ann Carter Lee who were prominent members of the Virginia aristocracy. My Mother was a descendant of one of the wealthiest families of Virginia and my Father, Light Horse Harry, had risen high, having served as the Governor of Virginia, been a member of the Congress of the United States, and also had earned the respect and friendship, not only of the men he commanded, the men of Lee's Legion of

Cavalry, but the Commander-in-Chief of the American Continental Army, General George Washington.

Unfortunately my Father made disastrous land speculations, squandering not only his own monies, but also my mother's. Things got so bad for him that for a while he spent some time in debtor's prison. In his prison cell Harry Lee wrote his memoirs of the Continental War. When he got out of prison my family moved to Alexandria where we lived on my Mother's modest legacy. Soon after, my father once more left us when he sought relief from wounds, obtained in the Revolutionary War, in the warmth of the West Indies. I never saw him again.

Later on, missing his family, he tried to get home but could not and died in the home of the daughter of his former army commander, Nathaniel Greene, in Cumberland, Georgia. May God rest his soul.

By now my dear mother was an invalid. But though she suffered severely, she spent many hours teaching me discipline, self-control, thrift, and most importantly, *honor*.

And it was *honor* that made me resign my commission when South Carolina seceded from the Union, and my home state, Virginia soon followed.[1]

President Lincoln, on the recommendation of General Winfield Scott, asked me to assume command of the Federal Army. This I had to refuse as I felt I could not raise my sword against my home state. Very soon after that the American Civil War began. It was then that I resigned my commission and joined the Confederate Army. With a lump in my throat and a shaking hand I began to write my resignation. As I wrote more than one tear fell to my cheeks. The following is my resignation letter:

To General Winfield Scott
Commander-in-Chief,
United States Army
Arlington Washington City P.O.
April 20, 1861
General Scott:

---

1 At first, on April 4, 1861 Virginia voted to stay in the Union, 90 to 45. After Fort Sumter, the Virginia Legislation re-voted, 80 to 55 to leave the Union.

Since my interview with you on the 18th instant I have felt that I ought no longer retain my commission in the Army. I therefore tender my resignation, which I request you will recommend for acceptance.

It would have been presented at once, but for the struggle it has cost me to separate myself from a service to which I have devoted all the best years of my life & all the ability I possessed.

I shall carry with me to the grave the most grateful recollections of your kind consideration & your name & fame will always be dear to me.

Save in the defense of my native state, I never again desire to draw my sword....

Most truly yours,

R.E.Lee

History is a nightmare from which I'm trying to awake

James Joyce

Chapter 2: Cheat Mountain

After the Confederate army lost Rich Mountain in West Virginia to the Union General McClellan, I was called by the leaders of the Confederacy away from my job as military advisor to President Davis, and sent to Cheat Mountain also in West Virginia. I was sent there to help General William Loring, the commander of the Army of Northwestern Virginia, to reclaim this rugged but important territory. Our main concern for this adventure was to safeguard the railroads of the Confederacy, namely the Virginia Central, and the Virginia and Tennessee railroads.

Cheat Mountain was a key position in West Virginia and controlled, not only railroads, but passage on a major turnpike along with several mountain passes.

The Union commander, Brigadier General Joseph Reynolds had only seven regiments on the mountain, but he had built and maintained a very strongly fortified post on Cheat Mountain. The Confederate General Loring had 15,000 men under his command and outnumbered the Federals severely but I didn't know that at the time.

On September 11th when our troops got to the mountain, it began to rain. That was an omen of things to come. On that fateful morning I had a conference with all of the officers under the command of Brigadier General Loring and carefully explained my battle plan to the officers present.

To begin the assault our men were to split their forces and attack the summit of Cheat Mountain with one brigade and at the same time a second brigade was to charge the remaining Union forces on the turnpike.

Although the rain never stopped, the next day we began our attack. Part of our forces made contact with the Union forces but soon broke off the charge because of the well-placed Union entrenchment and the Confederate Soldier's inexperience.

On September 12th, the next morning, we began again to try and implement my plan. General H. R. Jackson was to create a diversion along the Staunton-Parkersburg Turnpike in front of the Cheat Mountain fortifications. Meanwhile Colonel Albert Rust and his troops took a small back route up the mountain. A third body of men led by General Anderson was to lead his detachment along a trail discovered by myself. The sound of Colonel Rust's guns were supposed to initiate the massed assault. Unfortunately the rain continued its steady downpour and the Federal pickets discovered Rust's men. By the time our boys charged the summit and the turnpike, they were drenched and slipping and sliding in the mud on the mountain, not to mention that they were exhausted, and by this time, dispirited and also very hungry.[2] Discretion was the better part of valor and we

---

2 The Confederate soldiers had not yet learned to fight wet, hungry and xhausted, as they would successfully many times in the future

decided to abandon that part of the battle plan.

Trying to salvage the day, I then ordered an assault on Elkwater, the headquarters of General Reynolds. This was to be led by the last owner of Mount Vernon, Colonel John Washington my aide de camp. Unfortunately he was killed while on a pre-battle scouting expedition for me.

On all fronts, General Reynolds troops repelled our troops fairly easily. My summation was that our soldiers were too weak and hungry to fight with elan.

Most unfortunately, I made two foolish errors. First, I believed the Union soldiers we had captured when they told me we were outnumbered two to one. The second mistake I made was that the raw Confederate Soldiers and their inexperienced officers would be unable to understand the complex military plan of my attack. (Much less do it in the mud.)

The result of my errors on that day was that the boys on the turnpike did make a spirited attack but the failure of the other pincer in the dual surprise assault on the summit never came off and my plan quickly fell apart. As a last resort I tried a flanking movement on the Federal right but they were too well dug in for us to succeed

On the next day, September 13th, we began to try another assault. But the Confederate soldiers were all still wet, hungry and exhausted. Also during the night Reynolds had received reinforcements and they had dug in solidly. Of course by then we had lost the element of surprise so I called off any try at the summit and ordered that we leave the field.

My casualties were light (about 100) but we had not inflicted much damage to the enemy either. I had to face the fact that because of the rain and the inexperience of the soldiers, my battle plan was a failure.

However all was not lost as I learned some very valuable lessons on those three wet days. I was not to repeat those mistakes at the Seven Days and Second Bull Run.

When I got back to Virginia, I soon realized the Southern Population and the newspapers thought the entire affair was a failure also. To my dismay, I began to hear the whispers of "Granny Lee" when I passed. To further my humiliation President Davis shipped me off to supervise fortifications on the South Carolina coast. I thought seriously then of resigning, believing that my military career was over.

War, the mad game the world so loves to play

Jonathan Swift

Chapter 3: The Battle of Seven Pines

After the fiasco at Cheat Mountain in West Virginia, I was in the doldrums spending my time supervising the building of fortifications along the coasts of South Carolina and Georgia. But then President Davis sent for me. He met with me, at the Confederate White House, to plan the strategy for General Jackson in the Shenandoah Valley. Therefore I got to exercise my strategic muscle advising General Thomas (Stonewall) Jackson in his valley campaign. As you now know, my plans were sound, and due to the brilliance of General Jackson in carrying out the strategy, the battles were a colossal success. Several Yankee armies were routed and the whole business, together with his brilliant stand at Bull Run, described by General Bee, vaulted General Jackson to everlasting fame. As for myself I was content to remain in the background and gain satisfaction of my job well done.

A short time later I was suddenly summoned to the Confederate White House once more and quickly brought to President Davis.

The President, looking wan and ill, bade me to have a seat and I did so. For a few moments he paced behind his desk then he stopped and with a dour look said, "On the 31st of May, General Johnston was seriously wounded at Fair Oaks!"

He stopped and stared at me trying to discern my reaction. I gave none but inside I tensed in anticipation.

"General Gustavus Smith was next in line for command and indeed he took over." The president then shook his head sadly. "But I'm sorry to say Smith commanded the Confederate Army in front of Richmond as if he were a duck that had been knocked senseless by a mallet. Our entire front is now in disarray." The president stared directly at me his black eyes boring into my soul. "Our boys are hanging on by their fingernails and I am biting mine."

Davis then walked over to me and put his hand on my shoulder. "General Winfield Scott said you are the finest soldier in the entire Federal Army. I know General Scott and when he says something I believe him."

President Davis then turned away from me and started pacing again. Suddenly he stopped and once more stared at me his eyes piercing and dark and his brow furrowed. The next few words he uttered were like gunshots bouncing off the walls of the Southern Whitehouse. "Will you now take over Johnston's army, stop those blasted Yankees, and drive them into the James River?"

In a bit of shock at the news I blurted out, "What happened to General Johnston?"

President Davis closed his eyes and shook his head. "Some damned Yankee put a bullet through his shoulder, and then to add to the misery an errant shell hit Johnston in the chest and knocked him clear off his horse." Davis' eyes opened again and bore into me once more. "Will you take over for him?"

Full of immense pride I immediately stood up and said, "Mr. President, I will proceed to the front and do my duty to the best of my ability."

In a few minutes I was dashing through the Richmond streets on horseback my mind racing with the possibilities of driving the Yankees away from Richmond, and indeed, clear out of Virginia. When I got to my home, there was my dear Mary moving about slowly telling Mildred where to plant her prize roses.[3]

As I dismounted I felt a sharp pain down my left arm and a dull heaviness in my chest. Stopping the dismount while holding on to the pommel of the saddle, I waited until the pain passed. The feeling of dread did not pass quickly and I felt weary as my feet touched the ground.

Mary ignored me but Mildred was more observant. She came to my side with a furrowed brow. "Father, are you all right?"

Ignoring the recent bout of arm pain, I leaned over and kissed my eldest daughter on her cheek. "I'm fine Mildred, and I have some news." Mary was now quite aware of what just

---

[3] Lee's wife Mary was already feeling the effects of arthritis that was to plague her throughout the war.

happened to me and gave me an anxious look. I smiled at her, took her arm and we all went inside. When I explained what had taken place at the Confederate White House, both women looked at me with pride. That bolstered me and I smiled as I went upstairs to pack.

Confederate President Jefferson Davis

I worked night and day for twelve years to prevent the war, but I could not. The North was mad and blind, (and) would not let us govern ourselves.

Do your duty in all things and never do less

Robert E. Lee

Chapter 4: The Confederacy strikes back

When I got to the front, the first thing I noticed was the terrible odor that I had not smelled since Mexico. It was from the dead still unburied in the swamps and forests. There were other soldiers from both sides that had died of their wounds and had been buried in shallow graves with a thin covering of earth that had quickly washed away with the rain.

To find out how the Federal army was positioned, I immediately called an officers meeting for a conference. The first officer, speaking at length, filled me in as follows:

On May 31st the Union Commander General McClellan had reached the suburbs of

Richmond at Fair Oaks, and there started to gather his strength for a final push into Richmond. Here is an order that was then read to his men:

Soldiers of the Army of the Potomac! I have fulfilled at least a part of my promise to you. You are now face to face with the Rebels who are held at bay in front of their capital. The final decisive battle is at hand. The result cannot be for a moment doubtful. Upon your valor, discipline and mutual confidence the result depends. General McClellan, Commanding

The other officers mostly told me of the position of their men and how many killed and wounded they had suffered. The last officer to speak, General Heth, said the following:

"Looking for a way to strike back at the Union Army before they swept over Richmond, General Johnston sent scouts out trying to find a weakness in General McClellan's formations. A scout named Harrison (later of Gettysburg fame) found two of the Federal corps, under General Porter, that appeared isolated on the south side of the Chickahominy River. General Johnston wasted no time in organizing his Divisions to take advantage of that situation. In a short while, giving McClellan no warning, General Johnston sent his forces careening into the Federal superior numbers opposing him on the Chickahominy River. Although the Confederate units attacked in an uncoordinated fashion, their audacity and fierce desire to win the day was enough to inflict severe casualties on the Federal army and succeed in driving them back.

Both armies then fed reinforcements into the battle and after sustaining numerous casualties on both sides each of them stabilized their positions.

On June 1st after a small defensive skirmish, General Johnston again sent his Confederate Army forward in a full attack on the Federal lines at Seven Pines. Initially though, the Confederates were late in organizing the start of the battle, but when they finally got completely organized, they pushed the Yankees back to their secondary defensive positions at Seven Pines. Then, after being reinforced, General A.P. Hill began a second push and the Federals again retreated. When the Federals also got reinforcements from the Union 2nd corps they halted their retreat and dug in where they were. With the additional firepower the Yankee line stood firm and the Confederate forces also had to halt and dig in. The battle was now a stalemate.

With both armies deadlocked and night coming on, one would suppose the days work was done. Not so on that day. Everyone's blood was up and both sides kept firing at each other. Unfortunately for the Confederacy, around twilight General Johnston was struck simultaneously in the right shoulder by a bullet and in the chest by shrapnel."

"I know," I said, "President Davis told me about that unhappy incident."

General Heth continued. "Unable to continue General Johnston was replaced by General Gustavus Smith. In two days, Smith became indisposed and was apparently not up to taking General Johnston's place."

General Heth gave me a formal salute and as I saluted back he said, "That concludes my report, sir."

I thanked the officers and sent them back to their men while I went to the headquarters tent and opened the maps of the area.

On June 2nd a few of days after I replaced Smith, we again attacked the Union positions but they were still too well dug in. We gained no ground, and both sides suffered more dead and wounded. After the battle of Seven Pines I was appalled when I found out that we had lost 6,134 men, but pleased that we inflicted a serious damage to the Federals causing them a loss of 5,031 men.

For the first time I began to realize that I must not only get victories but that I must conserve my manpower. Compared to the numbers in the industrial North, the agrarian South simply could not compete. It was true that Southern men were born to the gun and the saddled horse but that would not make up for the disparity in numbers.

I knew General McClellan by now and I was sure that this effusion of blood on the field of Seven Pines would unsettle McClellan and would make him very cautious. Long after the war, I learned of the following note to his wife.

...I am tired of the battlefield, with its mangled corpses and poor wounded. Victory has no charms for me when purchased at such cost." [4]

George

---

[4]Both sides sent wires to their headquarters claiming victory but the most important result of the battle of Seven Pines was that the 11,000 battle casualties shook McClellan and the Union Government severely. While on the Confederate side, even though the South lost their most popular general to a bullet to the shoulder, two days later he was replaced by Robert E. Lee who eventually led the South to a stunning victory.

This war is not about slavery

Robert E. Lee

Chapter 5: The Seven Days

After the last battle, while listening to their reports, I asked each of the officers their opinions on what to do next. I was surprised to hear from almost every one of them that they wanted to pull back to the outskirts of Richmond; all they could talk about was McClellan's siege guns crawling closer and closer to Richmond. As the last of them was speaking and continuing to draw a dismal picture of defeat, I had had enough and shouted a hearty, "STOP!"

"Do you all want me to believe we are defeated before we fight? NO! We will start our battle for Virginia from right HERE! You are all dismissed until tomorrow at 4 a.m. when I will expect you at this tent with a detailed report on all the units under your command."

My job, as I saw it, was to mold this discordant, loose-knit group of men made up of the Manassas veterans, the defenders of Richmond and the green recruits coming in from Georgia, and Virginia, into my army.

It took me the good part of a month to put these men and their officers into proper military units. I began by stressing sobriety and discipline. One of my worst problems was that all these men, officers and enlisted, came from the same towns and were on a friendly basis. That had to stop and was quickly done by instant punishment for any infraction of military discipline. During that time I begged, borrowed, and stole uniforms for all the men under my command and made very sure all of them had enough to eat. Next I started on the command structure by sacking all the incompetents and began giving the men deserving officers who knew what they were doing. (Most of the new officers were West Point men.) It was a tedious job, but when I was done this army had changed. They were organized and disciplined and I was proud of every last one of them. It was then that I named this valiant group of men, the Army of Northern Virginia!

****

Slowly but surely I realized more and more that we had a helpful man right in the Federal army. Washington had sent General McClellan a detective by the name of Allan Pinkerton. He was giving McClellan explicit and detailed reports on how many men I had in the Army of Northern Virginia. The only problem for the Yankees was Pinkerton was telling McClellan I had upwards of two hundred thousand troops, or more – that gave us an advantage of more than two to one. This amount of men was of course, a ridiculous number. We had no army of that size nor were we able to get that many men. But the best thing for us was that McClellan believed him hook, line and sinker.

I realized that no matter how good my men were, there were only 60,000 of them, while arrayed in front of them, in a semi-circle, were a hundred thousand Federal Soldiers. So the opening move I made was to have my entire army dig in opposite the enemy.

For the next few days the men fought with pick and shovel until they had an earthworks system consisting of trenches, breastworks and redoubts for 8 miles from White Oak to the Chickahominy River. As soldiers will, they did grumble. Before long they were calling me, 'The King of Spades." Behind my back of course!

I thank God Almighty that while I was doing this training and entrenching for the better part of the month of June, we were facing General McClellan. Another more aggressive general might have overwhelmed us while I was getting my army ready to fight.

But I had an additional wrinkle in store for General McClellan. I knew he would stop where he was, start to bring up his big guns and then lay siege to Richmond, bombarding it into submission. Then he would carry the city by a frontal assault. I was so sure of his plan that while he was setting up his siege I wrote the following message to President Davis:

General McClellan will make this a battle of posts. He will take position to position under his heavy guns. But I am preparing a line that I can hold with part of our forces in front while with the rest I will endeavor to make a diversion which will ultimately bring McClellan out in the open.

R.E. Lee

I knew that few Southerners were as elated as my family was when I took over for General Johnston in the summer of '62. And despite all the naysayers in my own officer corps, in five weeks from the day I took over the army, by June 25th they were ready for anything the Federals could throw at them.

After losing ten percent of the army in the Seven Pines battle, the Confederate Army waited with bated breath to see if General McClellan would attack. But I knew my man, and I was confident that General McClellan wouldn't assault our depleted lines, so despite all expectations I prepared to attack him.

What I had in mind was while part of my army hunkered down with Generals Huger and Magruder in the recently dug trenches in front of Richmond, another part of my army would go north of the Chickahominy to cut off McClellan's supply line. But first I had to get better intelligence of the dispositions of the Union army. That's when I called in General Jeb Stuart.

From whence shall we expect the approach of danger?

Abraham Lincoln

Chapter 6: Stuarts Trip Round the Union Army

On June 12, 1862, I ordered General Stuart to select 1,200 men and several officers to scout and map the positions of McClellan's forces north of Richmond.[5]

Before he left, I suggested to General Stuart that he march north, make a feint toward Jackson in the Shenandoah Valley and

[5] This ride around McClellan's Army was just what Jeb Stuart lived for. The audacious Stuart strove for the limelight and now he had it. Among his force he chose a nephew of mine, Fitzhugh Lee, a 26-years-old colonel and a proven leader of men. Also he picked Colonel William Henry Lee (Lighthorse Harry Lee's namesake) the 25-year-old son of mine that everyone knew as *Rooney*.

then quietly turn east and proceed to a point behind General McClellan's right wing.

The next morning my son, Rooney Lee and his squadron ran into the Federal Fifth Cavalry. My son carried the day, but it was there that we lost the Gallant Captain Latané who led the final charge.

Continuing on Stuart gained more information about Federal positions while looting and burning Union supplies. He also, by this time had more than a few prisoners.

Here Stuart paused and made a fateful decision. He had come approximately halfway around the entire Federal Army. By this time the Union Soldiers were alerted to that fact and were lying in wait to ambush Stuart and his men as they tried to return back from where they had come.

Stuart called his officers for a conference. He spoke to them quietly telling them, "It would be less dangerous to continue on around McClellan's forces than it would be to go back from whence we came." His exact words, as was stated in his report were:

"It would be the quintessence of prudence to ride on and circle McClellan."

The officers agreed and they started off on the second half of their ride around McClellan's Army. This half proved to be more exciting than the first. Stuart's men had several battles, destroyed tons of Union goods and captured 165 Federal Soldiers. But all was not well because now they were being chased by Brigadier General Phillip St. George Cooke.[6]

Cooke almost caught them as they were building a bridge across the now raging Chickahominy River. But they got the bridge done, crossed it and then burned it just a few minutes before General Cooke arrived. I was told General Cooke jumped off his horse and slammed his hat to the ground as Stuart waved goodbye.

---

[6] General Cooke was General Stuart's father-in-law. In addition General Cooke's nephew was on Stuart's staff.

When he got back, to the adulation of all, Stuart gave me the maps he had made and reported to me. In his report was the good news that Porter's line was not anchored, and that I could precede with my plan of attack.

General Order No. 74

June 23, 1862
The general commanding announces with great satisfaction to the Army the brilliant exploit of General J.E.B. Stuart. This gallant officer, with portions of the First, Fourth, and Ninth Virginia Cavalry, a part of the Jeff Davis Legion, on June 13, 14, and 15, made a reconnaissance between the Pamunkey and Chickahominy Rivers, and succeeded in passing around the whole Federal Army, routing the enemy in a series of skirmishes, taking a number of prisoners, and destroying and capturing a large amount of stores... All this was done with but the loss of only one man.

In announcing this signal success to the army, the commanding general takes great pleasure in expressing his admiration of the courage and skill so conspicuously exhibited throughout by General Stuart and the officers and men under his command...
By the commanding General,
R.E. Lee

Not only did Stuart's ride build Southern moral but it exacerbated General McClellan's fears about losing his lines of supplies. More importantly Stuart's scouting revealed that McClellan's right wing, under Porter, was not anchored and vulnerable to assault.

Now it was my turn to attack. Gone would be the defensive maneuvering and torpor that characterized McClellan's style of fighting. I would attack them unmercifully until every last Federal lackey was driven from my native soil, my Virginia.

The key to my attack plan was Jackson's Army in the Shenandoah Valley. I sent my best courier to him immediately and ordered

Jackson to march his army to Richmond, but to leave a scratch force in place to hold General McDowell from leaving the Shenandoah Valley and coming to the support of McClellan. I also urged Jackson to ride ahead of his army and come for a meeting with me and the other generals involved in my plan of routing McClellan. The other generals in the meeting would be A. P. Hill and D. H. Hill, and their commander, General James Longstreet.

When a tired Jackson got to the meeting, I got up and addressed my officers. I stressed that everything depended on Jackson's "foot cavalry" being in position facing the right of McClellan's Army. I knew Jackson's men would be tired from their long march but it was imperative that as soon as General Jackson's men got in position they would have to attack. The gunfire from their attack would be the signal for Longstreet to begin his assault and together they would force the Yankees back to the James River.

My biggest problem then was that before everyone was in position all I had facing the 75,000 man Federal Army in front of Richmond was General John Magruder and his 20,000 men. My ace in the hole was knowing "Prince John", as Magruder was called, loved to act. I told him he was going to be on the greatest stage of his life. He was to be outnumbered 3 to 1 but he was to stage a show of force that indicated he was preparing to assault the Union line.

I must report he did his job to perfection by lighting multiple campfires, putting up countless tents, and marching his men and guns in an endless circle of activity, raising dust and Cain.[7] Now I was free to go after the Federal troops led by General Fitz John Porter that was camped on our side of the Chickahominy. I assembled three quarters of my army, (57,000 men) left the rest with Magruder and attacked Porter. After a relentless, grinding battle, we drove Porter clear across the Chickahominy River and in turn forced McClellan to retreat.

My assault was just in time as McClellan had just started Hooker's and Kearny's troops to invade Richmond. That is when Magruder stopped them. Not with guns and bombs, but

---

[7] Magruder later told me he was very nervous, thinking if the Yankees caught on to him, their 70,000 would roll over him and take Richmond.

with his men doing a hundred things to let the Yankees think we had as many men that Pinkerton told McClellan we had.

Before I go on, let me tell you what I know about Pinkerton. Allan Pinkerton was born in Glasgow, Scotland. After a period of time protecting Lincoln, Pinkerton was hired as a scout by the Federals to get information on the number of troops that I had under my command.

Instead of the 60,000 troops I actually had, Pinkerton told McClellan I had upwards of 200,000.8 That, apparently, was why McClellan, who believed Pinkerton's reports as if they were the gospel, was so loath to attack us.

By a strange coincidence, at almost the same time we were to attack, General McClellan decided to advance his army a little closer to Richmond to set up his siege guns to bombard the Southern Capitol. He began his assault on the morning of June 25th and made some headway against stubborn resistance.

---

[8] Allan Pinkerton gained his reputation when he guarded Lincoln on his trip from Illinois to Washington, D.C. in 1861. As a result of that reputation, despite his grossly inaccurate information at Seven Pines, Pinkerton was selected to coordinate the Federal Secret Service.

After three hours of fighting, at the battle of Oak Grove, the Federals were less than five miles from Richmond. I watched the skirmish from in back of our lines worried that McClellan knew about our plan to attack, when suddenly the Federal Troops were inexplicably called back.

I breathed a great sigh of relief and thanked God for His continued generous mercy and for putting the reticent McClellan at the head of the Union Army, with Pinkerton as his advisor.[9]

It was after this battle that McClellan sent his famous (or infamous) letter to Lincoln and Stanton:

If I save this army now, I tell you plainly that I owe no thanks to you or to any other persons in Washington. You have done your best to sacrifice this army....[10]

---

[9] This small battle initiated the week of continuous bloody fighting on the peninsular that would evermore be known as "The Seven Days".

[10] When this message was received in the war department the clerk decoding dispatches couldn't believe this eye-popping dispatch. He was so shocked he immediately deleted the above sentences from the message

JEB Stuart

He never gave me a false piece of information

---

and sent it on. Fortunately Lincoln and Stanton did not see the contents of that letter until long after McClellan was gone.

The Confederate Congress eats peanuts and chews tobacco while my army is starving

Robert E. Lee

Chapter 7: The Battle of Mechanicsville

Now I was ready to attack McClellan's right flank. Longstreet was in position with his lead general, A. P. Hill, chafing at the bit to get at the Yankees. But where was Jackson? Then the message I didn't want came. It was from Jackson and it said he was bogged down and would be six hours late.

Six hours, I thought? It might as well be six days. Since I had no choice I told General Longstreet to tell everyone to stand down until Jackson's troops arrived.

After six hours, the commander of my newest division, General A. P. Hill, got impatient and thinking that Jackson should be nearby by now ignored my order, put on his flaming red battle shirt, a match for his red hair, beard and his disposition, and, instead of waiting for Jackson's attack, he began to assault the Yankees entrenched on the high ground behind Beaver Creek. Later he told me he thought Jackson should be close enough by now and come to the sound of the guns. He thought wrong.

To compound his being six hours late, when Jackson got to the battle area, instead of pitching in and outflanking the Federals, by all that was holy, instead of assaulting the enemy, he put his men in bivouac! Yes I said bivouac! And set up camp for the night. This surely was not the Jackson of the Shenandoah and later Chancellorsville.

I know his men were tired and had just marched for 120 miles but his inexplicable behavior gave the Federal Forces the upper hand and cost me 1,484 men, while the Federals under Porter lost only 361. The 44th Georgia alone lost 335 men out of 514 that were sent into the assault. We couldn't afford that kind of disparity for long.

Instead of dressing Hill down as he deserved, I was so distraught I simply held my head in my hands and almost wept.

As you can believe, I was deeply, bitterly disappointed by bad judgment, poor communications and most of all by General Jackson's performance. I began to realize right then that my officers did not always carry out my orders. That would have to change.

At the time I was very angry with both Jackson and Hill, but in the back of my mind I knew they were good officers, men whom I knew would be valuable in later battles. With that in mind, I voided the action of those two men in my official report by not mentioning Jackson's slowness and Hill's attacking without support and not notifying me before he charged. The only positive result of the battle of Mechanicsville for me was that McClellan began to withdraw his troops further down the peninsular and after that, never again gained the initiative.

President Abraham Lincoln

A house divided against itself cannot stand

No, if destruction be our lot, we must ourselves be its author

---

Abraham Lincoln

Chapter 8: The Battle of Gaines Mill

The next day it was a different story. Though the Federals held their ground against our repeated assaults I had a deep feeling that our aggressiveness was having a telling effect on General McClellan. He knew as well as I did that his long supply train was vulnerable to attack and that there were Confederate Soldiers in his rear. A captured Yankee confirmed my thinking by confessing that he was a messenger carrying dispatches to all the Federal Unit Commanders to gather up their men and supplies and make a concerted march to the James River, where the army would be protected by the cannons on the Union Gunboats.

At dawn on the 27th of June, Fifth Corps Commander, General Fitz-John Porter was ordered to leave the Federal position at Beaver Dam and withdraw to a new line behind a marshy creek called Boatswain's Swamp. Again the Federals arrayed themselves in an arc with Yankee artillery behind them poised to protect the Chickahominy bridges from Confederate assault.

With McClellan retreating, I felt emboldened to take advantage of the situation and attack him. Scouting the enemy, I realized that General Porter's entire corps was isolated north of the Chickahominy and subject to complete destruction. A. P. Hill was again my center with Longstreet on the right and Jackson on the left. Or so I thought. When I checked, I found that Jackson was again tardy and did not show up until late in the afternoon. One of my officers later said, "On this day Jackson was not really Jackson. He must have been under a spell."

Not willing to wait for Jackson, I again sent General A. P. Hill and also D. H. Hill in a joint assault. To my eternal frustration they did not attack simultaneously, but did it disjointedly and were beaten off by the Federals decisively. That incoherent assault cost us some of the highest casualties of the war.

General Longstreet was ordered in to help the two Confederate Divisions already fighting, but the Federal position was so strong all the new divisions gained were more casualties.

By five in the afternoon my officers were still sending their men in piecemeal. After watching them mess up my plan, I began to personally take charge of the assault. Exerting myself to the fullest, I slowly but surely organized the men to coordinate for an all-out assault. Just as I was finishing aligning the men, General Jackson rode up and saluted.

"Ah, General Jackson, I'm very glad to see you," I said a bit sarcastically. "I had hoped you would have been with us earlier." Jackson answered a bit sheepishly that he and his men would do anything that was necessary for victory. I thanked him and quickly went over the battle plan.

Just at twilight, Jackson and his men were ready. I immediately gave his men verbal encouragement to pitch into the

Federal Line, "We must free Virginia and the South," I said. Then General Jackson addressed his men. In a low menacing voice he just said, "Give them the bayonet." His men went hoarse cheering their leader. General Ewell waited until the men ended their cheer and then raised his sword and yelled, "Follow me!" and led the charge toward the Yankee line.

The baldheaded Ewell was a fighter and soon had his boys clawing their way ahead with Jackson just at the rear of them, watching for slackers and urging the boys from Georgia into the fray.

Finally at 7 p.m. I had everyone organized and we launched a full-scale attack supporting Jackson and Ewell. The battle raged back and forth around the Chickahominy for some time. At one point during the battle I lost hope for a few minutes when I watched the boys from Georgia storm a salient I particularly wanted to capture. After they were repulsed, I rode over and dismounted. I shook hands with many of the wounded and then addressed those still able to fight. I spoke to them with emotion, telling them how important getting this salient was. That did the trick. Suddenly the men from the 41st Georgia started running across the field howling the Rebel Yell.

But it was not over yet. The Federal soldiers defending the salient, all as dressed in blue as the winter sky, stood just behind their trenches as silent as the grave. There came not a sound from any one of them.

General Longstreet, standing by my side muttered solemnly, “I don’t like that silence. They are showing no fear.”

When our men reached the Federal line they met a stonewall of Union men, their left eyes glaring at our charging boys their right eyes hidden by the sights of their raised muskets. Suddenly I heard the sounds of cannon and three hundred muskets firing as one that mowed down the first line of our boys as if they had been sliced by a scythe. In just a few moments the smoke from the Federal rifles and cannons had mostly lifted and remained suspended like a blue, misty canopy 15 feet above the trenches. Through that bluish mist I could see my men lying at the feet of the first line of the reloading Yankee Soldiers. In a moment, a second line of Federal cavalry reached over them and continuing to fire at our boys, their carbines spitting death.

But those men from Georgia were too determined to quit. Line after line of them came on and soon even the bravest of Yankees had to retreat taking their cannons with them. But they did so in order, and even retreating they took an additional toll of our boys. It was bravery and the ultimate of honor on both sides. I give all thanks to God in his highest Vault in Heaven that eventually we prevailed. Our boys took the trenches and the Federals retreated across the marshes.

Fortunately for the Yankees, only darkness prevented a total Union catastrophe. Under cover of night and a totally exhausted Confederate Army, General Porter got the remnants of his drained and weary army across the Chickahominy River and then burned the bridges behind them.

I must take a moment here to praise the generalship of General Porter and the surprising but remarkable bravery and tenacity of the Union Troops. The final total of casualties tells of the gallantry and valor on both sides. It was a resounding Confederate Victory, but I must add that the victory was costly. The Battle of Gaines Mill cost the Union 6,837 casualties including 2,836 captured. But, God help us, we lost 8,751 men in the fray. More importantly, although it showed their total commitment and bravery, among the dead were many of our brigade and regimental commanders. This turned out to be a serious problem in future actions as I had no quick way to replace those valued and respected men.

There was one more thing. I noticed that before, during and after the battle, there was a Union balloon hovering over the battlefield. If McClellan had taken advantage of the knowledge the balloonist had gained of the number of our troops and their movements, the outcome of the battle might have been different.

Winfield Scott Hancock

I do not care to die, but I pray to God that I may never leave this field

There is a tide in the affairs of men

Shakespeare

Chapter 9: The Battle of Golding's Farm

On June 27th Brigadier General Magruder who had been fooling the Union troops at his front with theatrical diversions soon found the troops he was deceiving had left their trenches. He notified me and I ordered General Magruder to find out where McClellan's troops had gone. He, in turn, ordered General Toombs' brigade to move forward and perform a reconnaissance.

Unfortunately, General Toombs was a politician and not a professional soldier. When he found the retreating Federals, instead of informing his commander he ordered an attack. I later found out he attacked Brigadier General Winfield Scott Hancock. He was no match for Hancock and in his haste to win glory he lost 271 Georgians.

On June 28th, Toombs was again ordered to scout the Union Army and report back to his commander. Instead of doing that, when he found the Federals at Golding's Farm he again disobeyed orders rushing into another attack on the Federal Army. But this time he compounded the error by ordering Brigadier General Anderson's troops to join him in the assault. The Federals not only stopped the Confederate attack but in a counterattack caused the loss of another 156 Confederate men.

The result of this mismanaged battle at Golding's Farm was Union casualties: 189, Confederate: 438. A foolish misuse of Georgia men, yes, but, this fiasco had a bright side. General McClellan now had been attacked from the south of the Chickahominy and felt he was being assaulted from several directions. This increased his anxiety to get his army to the safety of his gunboats on the James River and he ordered his men to march there with all deliberate speed.

When the government fears the people, there is liberty

Thomas Jefferson

Chapter 10: The Battle of Savage's Station

On June 29th 1862, the two armies were destined to meet at Savage Station, Virginia. It was the fourth battle of the Seven Days Campaign of the Civil War.

That morning found an anxious General McClellan withdrawing toward the James River. I found out later that General McClellan himself had moved on south after the Battle of Gaines Mill without leaving verbal or written instructions for Federal Corps movements. Inexplicably and incredibly, he also left no one in command for the Federal retreat to the James.

In addition, there were 2,500 wounded men lying around in a field hospital in various stages of injury who soon knew they would not be evacuated from Savage Station with the rest of the army. This did irreparable harm to the morale of the wounded and to their comrades who had to leave them.

By this time I received a very strange visitor. Unbeknown to me, General Johnston had formed a Confederate Balloon Corps led by Captain John R. Bryant. That gentleman was my visitor. I was astounded to now know that we will have our own balloonist above the battle area and that I also will receive messages of the Union Army movements from Captain Bryant. I immediately sent Captain Bryant off to his balloon and told him to get it aloft by seven the next morning.

After studying the maps and the terrain of Savage Station I began to realize that if we hurried we could get around the Federal Army, surround it and defeat it in detail. I made a new plan to cut off the Federal Army from reaching the James by attacking them from two sides in a pincer movement.

I immediately sent for and ordered General Magruder to follow the retreating

Yankees, find the Federal rear guard and, without waiting for orders, strike them at Savage Station. While Magruder was attacking, General Longstreet and General A. P. Hill were to loop around back toward Richmond then cut across to Glendale completing a pincer move that would force the Federals to fight while retreating.

During this move General Magruder was supposed to be supported by General Jackson. Unfortunately, as he had been before, General Jackson was late for the assault. He was stuck near the Chickahominy and could not join Magruder's attack. Jackson's orders were to rebuild a bridge over the Chickahominy River and then immediately link up with Magruder. But Jackson was nowhere in sight. My order for him to join in with the Magruder attack was not obeyed. Instead he got another confused order that had his troops rebuilding bridges and then, instead of fighting Yankees, they guarded the bridges. Clearly the Jackson of the Seven Days was not the Jackson of Bull Run, the Valley and Chancellorsville.

When General Magruder caught up with the Union rear guard they were two miles from Savage Station. The two armies fought for two hours with the Confederates suffering 28 casualties while the federals lost 119.

Uncharacteristically, General Magruder walked about confused, mumbling about a superior force attacking him, and where is Jackson?

With or without Jackson, Magruder had some other firepower. I had supplied him with a 32 pounder Naval Brook rifle that could be used to counter McClellan's siege guns. The soldiers named it the, "Land Merrimack". Magruder put it into action as soon after he found the Union Army.

Magruder's army was small, but the Union's General Sumner did not utilize his men properly. This resulted in a very bloody stalemate. Both sides lost 1,500 men, not counting the 2,500 wounded left at the evacuated Union field hospital. But despite the powerful gun he had Magruder was not aggressive and Sumner retreated right under Magruder's nose.

When I found out that most of the Federal Army of the Potomac had escaped, I sent General Magruder a dispatch showing my disgust at letting the Federals escape:

I regret much that you have made so little progress today in the pursuit of the enemy. In order to reap the fruits of our victory that pursuit should have been most vigorous... (In the future) We must lose no more time or he will escape us entirely.

General R.E.Lee

James Longstreet

No 15,000 men can take that hill!

One man with courage makes a majority

Andrew Jackson

Chapter 11: The Battle of Frayser's Farm

When we got the Federal Army to retreat from Savage Station, they got across the White Oak Swamp River just north of Glendale, Virginia. I then ordered Jackson, A. P. Hill and Longstreet to cross the Chickahominy after them. Generals Huger and Magruder had been responsible for holding the bulk of the Union Army at bay since the battle of Mechanicsville and, other than being a bit slow at times, had done an admirable job. Keeping General Huger and his excellent South Carolinians on active duty, I ordered General Magruder's men to be relieved and sent to the rear for rest and refitting. I then ordered General Jackson to pursue the army under the Federal General Edwin Sumner. Sumner wisely chose a natural obstacle for defense, a river. The White Oak River was wide at the point that the Union Army set up its defensive position and provided them a natural barrier that would be difficult to assault. In addition to that, other Federal Forces began arriving there adding to our difficulties. But here was another opportunity to trap a good portion of the Union Army. I ordered General Huger to move around the Federals and trap them, but, as happened so many times before in the "Seven Days" Huger got overly careful.

On the late afternoon of June 29th, a scout brought him word that the one-arm, but always dangerous, General Phil Kearny was preparing to cross the White Oak Swamp River at Jordan's Ford, immediately in front of General Huger's troops. Believing the information to be reliable, Huger, without my knowledge, stopped where he was, dug in and waited for Kearny. He waited in vain as Kearny had been at Jordan's Crossing hours earlier, thought the crossing was to wide and deep for his troops, and crossed the White Oak Swamp river at a bridge far down river.

During all this activity, as I said before, the Commander of the Federal Troops, General McClellan inexplicably had left the field, and even more bizarre, he left without giving command to a subordinate. I have never heard the reason he was at Haxall's Landing, which is east of Harrison's Landing, or just why he had simply left his troops.

I repeat, why he chose not to be at Harrison's Landing, which was the safe destination for his army is beyond my understanding.

However his army was not safe yet since I had my troops at the Union Army's heels snapping and biting as hard as they could. I figured if I could destroy the entire Federal Army, Washington itself might fall to us. Then we had a chance to get Lincoln and perhaps even the Union Congress to sue for peace.

This was our opportunity. And I could hardly believe it but for once, at the battle of Glendale, we had more men than the Yankees. My plan was again to split my forces, sending Holmes around the Federal Army, which was camped at their site on Malvern Hill, while Huger's South Carolinians and Jackson's Army of the Shenandoah Valley went around to the other side and closed the pincer movement. I could see the end of the war from where I stood. Alas, Just when I could see the end, God seemed to desert us. It was not to happen!

Now, I thought, I had the Federal Army on the run and I wanted to make the most of it. To make sure everyone understood my plan I called the three generals together. At that meeting I ordered General Holmes to proceed to the left of the Federal encampment on Malvern Hill and generals Huger and Jackson to go to the right and surround the unsuspecting Federal Army.

Sadly once again Jackson failed me, and Huger did no better. They both arrived late at Malvern Hill, and until they arrived, General Holmes faced the entire Union Army alone. When the tardy Jackson finally arrived, he was close to the Federal wagon train of supplies and all of the Federal supplies were in jeopardy of being taken by his troops. At first the Federals panicked, but then realizing their lives and well-being depended on their supplies, they hunkered down, dug in and faced Jackson. With the added incentive of saving their supplies the Federal Army prepared to fight off my troops, and they did!

To compound my problems, an exhausted General Jackson, after chasing the Union Army from Savage Station for 12 hours, instead of pitching into the Yankees, unbelievably and inexplicably sat down under an oak tree and fell asleep. And he was not difficult to wake once he fell asleep, he was impossible!

To further add to my difficulties President Davis arrived on the field. Having once before told him, unceremoniously to leave the field during a battle, this time I thought better of it, swallowed my pride, and asked the president for his advice. While he discussed his views, General Longstreet joined us. I listened carefully to both men and solidified my plans in my head. When the President left I bade General Longstreet goodbye telling him to get some rest as I had work for him to do in a short while. I then proceeded to headquarters tent and roused Majors Taylor and Venable to take down my battle plans and deliver them to my officers.

While I was thus organizing the Confederate Army for an attack on the retreating Federals, a sweaty roan pulled up with an excited corporal on board. Without even bothering about military courtesy he leapt down from the horse and handed Major Taylor a dispatch. Then he stood at attention waiting for a reply. Taylor handed me the dispatch.

The note was from General Huger. It was simple but it made my stomach flip. He would be delayed! *Can my generals do anything right this week? How can I destroy the Federal Army with such incompetent officers?*

Of course I didn't say any of this out loud, but I must admit I was thoroughly disgusted with the command structure I inherited and thought, *I must do something about getting competent officers.*

Another messenger galloped up just then, jumped off his horse, saluted and handed me a second dispatch. It was more bad news. General Holmes wrote:

The Union Columns are now moving past Malvern Hill and would soon be protected by the Federal gunboats on the James River.

It was now or never! I crushed the paper in my fist and turned to Major Taylor. "Get me General Longstreet." The major turned and started to leave and I called after him, "He may be asleep but wake him anyway he must be ready to lead his men right away."

When he got to me I ordered General Longstreet to assault the Union line just ahead at Glendale. When I went to view the attack, I couldn't believe what I saw. Longstreet fed his troops in piecemeal, replacing fresh men in as the previous men tired. I said nothing to Longstreet but I thought at the time: *This place, Frazier's Farm, will go down in history as the place of lost opportunity!*

Unfortunately for us, Longstreet's troops faced the competent General Meade, backed up by the equally competent Generals Joe Hooker, Phil Kearny and Fitz-John Porter.

As the battle progressed, I saw General Longstreet on horseback sweeping across the Federal line probing for a soft spot. He found a few but the Federal men realizing if they allowed the Confederates to get to their supply wagons they would be finished, fought like furies. And they didn't need to close the gaps and push my army back – their cannons did the work for them.

It was then that I made a serious error. Instead of staying near Frazer's Farm and urging my troops on, I left the battlefield and personally went to look for a way around the Yankees to flank them. This is what I had done in the Mexican War that worked so well at Cerro Gordo. But this was not Cerro Gordo and my search for a path around the Federals was a waste of time, and I found out later a waste of men.

In the meantime, at midday, General Hooker found a place to put his artillery and began to enfilade our lines. That and an infuriated General Kearny standing just behind his men sword in hand urging his men to protect their homes and property. It was enough and we had to move back.

This final battle against the cream of the Federal general staff was devastating to us and we retreated with great loss.

It was now 8:30 in the evening and in the dusk two things happened to end the day. First, in the ensuing darkness, the Union General McCall got lost. He saw a company of men and called out, "Who is your commanding officer?" When they answered in a South Carolina drawl he knew he was captured.

The second thing happened just after his capture. As night fell both armies let out huge cheers signifying the end of a trying day, not only for the troops but exhausting me to the point where I was breathing hard and had some chest pains. To have come so close to destroying the Federal Army and ending the war, and to lose that opportunity by incompetence was dismaying. Now the Federals will re-arm, re-fit, rest up and come after us again.

Even in the dark some soldiers on both sides had not had enough. One Union Colonel made a final charge and since no one could see, both sides fired at the flashes of the enemy's rifles. Finally, when that charge failed, silence crept over the battlefield and all was quiet. That is, all was quiet except the horrible cries of the wounded that lasted all night.

One area on both sides was still busy. The Union Generals met to discuss the best way to get their army to the James River while I spoke to my officers about the best way to stop them.

When McClellan had his army more safe and secure, I spent a great deal of time reliving the Seven Days of carnage. The question to myself was, what had gone wrong? The answers were as follows:

First, I inherited men who were undisciplined and must be retrained militarily.

Second, my officers were ignorant of military necessities, logistics and communications.

Third, I had to replace the incompetents and get or train knowledgeable commanders.

Fourth, my plan of converging cannon fire on Frazer's Farm and then a frontal charge was a sound plan. But it was not carried out properly. Confusion ruled, the cannon did not fire properly and the men attacked piecemeal. And worse than all of that, I was not there to see it through.

The time is near at hand which must determine whether Americans are to be free men or slaves

---

George Washington

Chapter 12: The Battle of Malvern Hill

On July 1st 1862, I made a serious mistake. The Federals on Malvern Hill had been up all night preparing their defense. It was the last day of the now famous Seven Days and I was proud of my troops and also of myself. Alas as the good book says, 'Pride cometh before a fall.'

Not only did Malvern Hill give the Yankees excellent observation for my troop movements and elevation for 250 Federal guns facing us but they were backed up by three large gunboats on the James River, The Galena, the Aroostook, and the Jacob Bell.

All three ships had large cannons that could easily reach beyond Malvern Hill.

As soon as the sun rose on July 1st, I trained my binoculars on Malvern Hill. What I saw there made my blood run cold. The Federals had cleared the slopes of timber giving them a clear field of fire in all directions with not only their rifles but the 250 cannons placed selectively by the excellent artillerist Colonel Henry Hunt. I also knew this was no amateur facing us, but General Fitz-John Porter, who obviously knew his business.

On top of all that we were now facing the entire Union Army arrayed in a large semi-circle. It was more, or less, like the fishhook formation later used by General Meade at Gettysburg.

I was faced with a fateful choice: either try to flank the Federal Army, or soften them up with Artillery and then make a head on assault. A search of the area previously had shown the terrain was swampy and heavily forested. This scouting report made a flanking movement less promising. That left me only one other choice to hit the Federal line head on. *Yes*, I thought, *one more push and we'll have them clear out of Virginia!*

My idea for the charge was as follows: the artillery would begin their bombardment first to clear the way. Then General Jackson and his Foot Cavalry were to lead the charge against Malvern Hill. General Magruder's men were ordered to follow up Jackson, then as they approached the battlefield they were to turn to the right. General Huger was to follow Magruder and then stop and wait for developments on the battlefield before he deployed his men. Longstreet and Hill were held in reserve as their men had been in exhaustive combat the day before.

I was approached by General D. H. Hill just before the battle was to commence. He shook his head and quietly said to me, "General Lee, in that position they are too strong. We should let them leave or find another way to fight them."

I thought for a moment and then answered him. "Napoleon did exactly the same thing at Austerlitz that we are going to do now, and he was successful. And we, God willing, will be successful too. Keep the faith General and trust to the Lord's will."

I am told that at Malvern Hill, I fed my men piecemeal and that is why we were decimated. This is not a true evaluation of the situation. My plan, although complex, was not followed in detail. My troops were delayed severely by incorrect maps, muddy roads and swamps. In addition, inexplicably, when Jackson got to his first swampy creek he stopped. This abrupt change in my plan threw everything else off schedule. Then Magruder was sent, believe it or not, AWAY from the battlefield by poorly informed scouts.

I now scrambled to put another force in place to make the charge. I put Huger's division on the right and D. H. Hill on the left. (Don't forget that Hill did not believe in the charge, but at that point I had no choice as I had no one left for that command. He did have John Bell Hood and Evander Law under him that made me feel somewhat secure.) Huger and Hill prepared to charge and waited only for OUR bombardment to begin.

Unfortunately for us, the Federal Artillery Commander Colonel Hunt struck first. From 1:00 p.m. until 2:30, he unleashed the largest artillery barrage known to warfare at that time. At the beginning of the barrage the Union gunners targeted and destroyed most of our artillery at Poindexter's farm. Then they turned their guns on the advancing Confederate columns getting ready for their charge. To my dismay those troops were blasted to pieces.[11] The most terrifying blows were the 50-pound shells unleashed by the three Union gunboats on the James River. Even from where I stood, when those shells hit the ground I could feel the earth tremble from the shock. God help the soldiers that went through that storm. Despite the calamity of the Union Artillery, at 3:30, one hour after the artillery barrage began I sent my regular troops forward with orders to take Malvern Hill.

Progress against the Union Line was made on the right by Generals Armistead and Wright. (Both of those men were to become deservedly famous at Gettysburg.) A half-hour later Magruder and his men arrived and I immediately ordered him forward to support Armistead.

---

[11] Half the Confederate casualties, in this battle were inflicted by artillery fire, an unknown before this war. Most men killed or wounded before this battle were victims of infantry muskets.

Damn and double damn! To this day every time I think about it my blood boils and my neck tightens up. Right in front of me Magruder attacked piecemeal instead of sending in his troops all at once. To me it was the most poorly organized attack of the Seven Days. Those poor boys under Magruder were soon cut to pieces.

In the meantime, D. H. Hill hurled his men toward the Union center, but as he had predicted, his men were repulsed with heavy loss.

Finally, as night was coming on, I saw General Jackson. He had just stopped General Trimble and his men and was talking to him heatedly.

"Where are you going, General?" I heard Jackson say.

Trimble pointed to the Union batteries. "I'm going to charge those batteries, Sir."

Jackson shook his head and said quietly, "I guess you better not try it."

"Why not?"

"Because General Hill just tried it with his entire division and has been repulsed. I guess you better not try it."

We had one more chance to do some real damage to the Federals, but once again poor judgment threw that chance away. On Evelington Heights we could have placed what was left of our artillery and looked down on the Union troops hunkered down in their camps. This would have made their position untenable. But along came General Jeb Stuart and with one single cannon began to bombard the Union camp. This alerted the Union commanders to their danger and they immediately sent up infantry troops and captured the heights.

The next morning was a gloomy day that greeted us with rain and dead men. All night long we had heard the cries of the wounded and dying and now we knew why.

At dawn that morning Federal Cavalry Colonel William Averel told it best. In his report he wrote about the battle aftermath:

I looked in horror through the morning mist at the slopes of Malvern Hill and saw what we had been hearing all night long. Dead and wounded men were on the ground in every attitude of distress. A third of them were dead or dying, but enough of them were alive and moving that gave the field a singular crawling effect.

My own thoughts of the Battle of Malvern Hill were, *It is well war is so terrible lest we learn to love it.* (I had the same thought at Fredricksburg when the shoe was on the other foot).

The wounds inflicted by the Union cannons were horrific. They were so effective that the Union infantry could have just been interested spectators.

On my way back to Richmond later that day I resolved to assert better command, improve the staff work, be more explicit in communications, improve tactics and insist on total discipline.

My first task though, was the rebuilding of my battered army

When I was told the total of our Malvern Hill casualties, I was appalled. Major Taylor informed me we had lost 5,650 men. (I was later told the Union lost only 2,214) But the real shock about our losses came when Taylor later said we lost 20,614 men overall, nearly one fourth of our Army. (Later I found that the Federals had lost only 15,849, a much lower percentage than us.)

At best, McClellan's army disappeared from the Virginia shores.

At worst, we had lost some of the South's best men[12] and even worse, a staggering toll of ten brigade commanders and 66 regimental commanders either killed or wounded.[13]

---

[12] What disappeared was the chance for a short war. The Seven Days battles were only a prelude for what was to come.

[13] Some of the men lost were the very best Confederate officers. More importantly, the loss of those officers was very costly in later battles.

I would free all the slaves to avoid this war

Robert E. Lee

Chapter 13: Aftermath of the Seven Days

By July 3rd, The Seven Days battles were done. The Federal Army was gone and Richmond was safe. But in my official report to the President and the Confederate Congress, I'm afraid I let my anger spill over about letting McClellan and the Union Army escape. In addition to praise for the Army of Northern Virginia, I noted the failures of my subordinate officers, and said in very plain English:

Under ordinary circumstances the Federal Army should have been destroyed.

General Orders No. 75

To President Davis:
The general commanding, profoundly grateful to the only Giver of all victory for the signal success with which He has blessed our arms, tenders his warmest thanks and congratulations to the Army of Northern Virginia, by whose valor such splendid results have been achieved.
On Thursday, June 26th, the powerful and thoroughly equipped army of the enemy was entrenched in works vast in extent and most formidable in character within sight of our capitol. Today, the remains of that confident and threatening host lie upon the banks of the James River, thirty miles from Richmond, licking their wounds and seeking to recover, under the protection of their gunboats, from the effects of a series of disastrous defeats.

The battles of the Seven Days are over,
won by men in heroic conduct
engaged in a cause so just and sacred,
and deserving of a nation's gratitude
and praise.
By Command of General Lee

I have come from the west where we always see the backs of our enemies

General John Pope

Chapter 14: The Battle of 2nd Bull Run (Manassas)

There was only one commander that I did not respect, in the Late Unpleasantness, and that was Pope. (Later, Pope's place in my anger was taken by Beast Butler.)

I respected General McClellan and appreciated General Grant. But after Pope bragged about his headquarters being, 'in the saddle', and the way he treated the Southern populous with his "proclamations", I determined if we ever met on the battlefield I would make sure he was defeated in detail.

What was his "proclamation"? Let me tell you:

Item 7 and 11 of the proclamation declared how his army was supposed to treat the civilian population. The first item stated that: All males who refused to sign an oath of loyalty to the Union would be arrested on sight with no trial, or exiled, (to who knows where.) Another item was: Any and all damage to Union military property will be charged to civilians who live within five miles of the damage.

After McClellan's defeat in the Seven Days Battles, President Lincoln, after observing Popes triumphs in the west, thought he had an aggressive general who could give him the victories he needed. What he really had was a pompous ass that our soldiers quickly and aptly changed his headquarters statement to: 'His hindquarters were where his headquarters should be.'

I know now that President Lincoln called Pope to Washington and gave him two objectives. First he was to protect Washington, and second he was to draw my forces away from McClellan by moving his army toward Gordonville. When my army went after Pope, then McClellan could attack my rear and I would be caught in a pincer. Good advice, but I knew my man and was fairly certain McClellan would not move swiftly. Based on my experience fighting McClellan during the Seven Days Battles, in all kinds of situations, I figured he would be very slow or not move at all. So, since I was confident that McClellan would remain idle I dispatched Jackson's and Richard Ewell's Divisions to block Pope's new Union Army called, The Army of Virginia.

Since I felt that McClellan would be little or no threat to my army, I detailed a simple curtain of my cavalry to keep an eye on McClellan while I dealt with Pope. Perhaps it was a serious gamble but I thought it was worth the risk. As slow as McClellan was during the Seven Days I felt a squadron of cavalry would be sufficient to watch him.

Pondering who to send on this important blocking mission I decided to talk to General Jackson to see if I could rely on him once again. His behavior during the Seven Days made me a bit reluctant to use him in this important blocking action, but I knew I would need him in the future and he did such a masterful job in the Shenandoah, I decided to take a chance.

I called him to my tent and laid out my plan. His interest and demeanor told me I was talking to the old Jackson and I now felt sure he could handle the task. The action was very important for not only was he to block Pope, but he would have to protect the Virginia Central Railroad, the bringer of our supplies and the mover of our men.

Since the Union Army was widely separated, my plan was to get between them, attack Pope and defeat him in detail and then, since I knew McClellan would move slowly or not at all, turn and assault him and finally destroy his army completely. Then, when I turned my army toward Washington, I prayed Lincoln would sue for peace and we could all go home again.

With all this in mind I called A. P. Hill to headquarters and ordered him to join in supporting Jackson in the blocking task. (As I had predicted the Union Chief in Washington, General Henry Halleck ordered McClellan to immediately join and support Pope.) Whether he did not join him at once because of his innate slowness or because he wanted Pope to be defeated I cannot say, but in my heart I believe the latter. In any event McClellan did not start his redeployment until August 14th, while Union forces under General Banks attacked Jackson on August 9th.

****

But first things had to come first. After the Seven Days ending at Malvern Hill both armies lay wounded and exhausted in the sweltering heat of a Virginia summer. I now undertook my main task that was a thorough reorganization of my army whose command structure had proven dangerously inadequate during the Seven Days battles. The eleven divisions I took over behaved like separate armies with no contact or coordination with the other divisions.

With the way things were, the only movements we made were patrols to make sure we weren't surprised by a sudden Yankee attack. I then ordered that the entire balance of the month of July was to be given over to rest, supply and military teaching of the now bloodied, but still green troops.

Meanwhile, since we were in the swampy lowlands, our doctors were given to treating and healing the men with the worst of our medical problems, malaria. Sometimes I think that malaria took more men then the Federals did.

After looking after the troops, I turned my thoughts to myself, and my generalship in the Seven Days. I know that we should have destroyed the Federal Army in several battles, and now I had to go over every facet of each battle to find out why that did not happen.

The first thing that came to me is that my men were really civilians in military clothing. They needed to learn military discipline and I so ordered it. Not only did I order discipline, but I personally observed my officers instructing their men. Needless to say the supervision paid off as the former ragtag bunch of men I inherited soon turned out to be the Army of Northern Virginia, probably the best fighting men in the world.

The next thing I considered was communication. So many of my orders went awry, or never got to the officer in charge, it caused units to be in one place when they should have been replacing a unit somewhere else leaving both units subject to destruction.

The next problem I faced was with the subordinate generals. The fact that I had to get between Generals Longstreet and Hill to prevent a sword fight tells the whole story. It seems that Hill got a newspaper story about leading his men in the Seven Days. Longstreet saw it differently and they argued. Soon the argument turned more violent and one of them slapped the other with his glove. The offended officer thought he had no choice but to accept the dueling offer and they set a time and place together with seconds. When I got wind of this nonsense I called both of them to the headquarters tent and gave them a severe tongue-lashing. "We have no time for this foolishness," I told them, "the whole Yankee Army is at our doorstep and Virginia, and indeed the whole South is facing ruin." After telling them if I heard any more about a duel I would replace them both and send them home they shook hands and left.

That was not all. Both of them and several of my other generals ignored orders and many times sent men in piecemeal when a mass charge would have won the day. In addition, much to my dismay, several times the generals were late, and in Jackson's case never did arrive. Equally important was the necessity to get rid of political officers and replace them with West Point graduates, or at least men who knew how to fight and how to teach.

Realizing that McClellan's Army was unreachable under the guns of the warships anchored in the James River, I pulled the army back toward Richmond. This got the men out of the swamps so they could avoid the malaria, and then be resupplied, fed and decently quartered without interference.

After the men were cared for, I took on the main task of restructuring the entire Confederate Army. During the battles of the Seven Days there were too many divisions in the Confederate Army. Militarily, the eleven divisions were far too unwieldy for me to exercise coordinated control. I wanted to have the divisions work cooperatively and in tandem so they could be quickly responsive to my orders. This meant reorganization and I set about to do just that. I organized the three wings mentioned above with Jackson, Longstreet and myself in command of each wing. General Stuart was put in over-all command of the cavalry for all three wings.

Now back to General Banks. He struck first, attacking Jackson on August 9th.

To my complete surprise, the political General Banks assaulted Jackson and drove him back to Cedar Mountain.

Expecting General McClellan to join him momentarily, Banks kept after Jackson hoping McClellan would quickly come and help destroy Jackson's small army. Acknowledging the surprising situation, I immediately ordered General Hill to join Jackson.

So it wasn't McClellan who came in for support it was A. P. Hill. And the support wasn't for the Yankees but for my Confederates. Taking just a moment to put on his flaming red battle shirt, Hill attacked Banks[14] and immediately changed the course of the battle. On the 13th of August, I sent my reserve, General Longstreet, to assist Jackson and Hill at Gordonsville. Due to the constant rain, the Rappahannock River was swollen and could not be crossed. Longstreet was

---

[14] Before the war, General Nathaniel Banks was a U.S. congressman and governor of Massachusetts. As a political appointee by President Lincoln, he was named a major general of volunteers. His battle career was rather dismal but his appointment served its purpose in rallying support of New Englanders (and more importantly the abolitionists) for the war effort.

stopped by nature. (*And perhaps by his own stubbornness!*)

Meanwhile more of the Federals were arriving and plans had to be changed. I called for Jeb Stuart and gave him a message to take to Jackson:

General Jackson:
Take half of your army and half of General Stuart's men and make a flanking move around Pope and cut of his line of communication, the Orange and Alexandria Railroad. He will then have to retreat and as Napoleon said, 'An army retreating in the face of an enemy is vulnerable'.
Your Obedient Servant,
R.E. Lee, Commanding

Jackson did as he was told and on the 25th, reached a good distance around Pope that night. The next evening, Jackson struck the Union force at Bristoe Station and captured the massive Union supply depot at Manassas Junction.

I have been told, and it's my impression, that the flamboyant Stuart had a field day at Bristoe Station. In his report, he said he cut the Union line to Washington, captured Pope's dress uniform and very importantly his dispatch books and to top it off several chests of Yankee payroll money.

General Pope, now knowing he had been cut off from Washington made an abrupt retreat from his defensive line along the Rappahannock.

Then, during the night of August 27–28, Jackson took advantage of Pope's retreat and marched his divisions north to the First Bull Run battlefield, where he took position behind a captured, unfinished railroad grade.

Jackson had picked an excellent defensive position as not only was his men concealed but there were good roads that would allow Longstreet to easily reach him. Also, he had good observation of Federal movements.

All of this worked well, as on August 28th, Longstreet broke through the Union resistance and joined Jackson, which according to my plan, assured Pope's defeat.

What happened was the following: Jackson attacked a Federal column just a short way from the town of Gainesville. The Federals fought like furies and the battle, called the Battle of Brawner's Farm, resulted in a draw. But on that very day, at Thoroughfare Gap, Longstreet smashed through a thin line of Union Soldiers and started marching, as he was ordered, to join Jackson.

Pope, thinking he had trapped Jackson in the railroad grade, lost no time in gathering the largest part of his army and began assaulting Jackson on the morning of August 29th. The attacks were furious but Jackson repelled them. However, Jackson was fighting the Iron Brigade that was being led by General John Gibbon, arguably the most competent General on the field. In this situation, there were serious losses on both sides and the battle ended in a stalemate.

During the worst of the heated battle, General Jackson ordered his horse artillery, under the command of Captain John Pelham, to move forward. Pelham met the enemy and both armies started firing at each other at less than 100 yards. Later I heard the usually silent Jackson shake his head and say, "It was a fierce and bloody battle."

Confederate Brig. General Taliaferro wrote:

In this fight there was no maneuvering and very little tactics. It was a question of endurance and both (armies) endured. Late in the battle my friend, and fellow general, Richard Ewell's left leg was shattered by a Minié ball. Unfortunately, the leg had to be amputated, removing him from action for the next ten months.

After he lost his leg, General Ewell never seemed to be the same aggressive general again. Instead of being his usually belligerent self, he seemed unusually reticent at Gettysburg.[15] I never knew if it was the wound

[15] On the second day at Gettysburg, General Ewell's lack of aggression on taking Culp's Hill cost General Lee the heights on the iconic third day.

at Brawner's Farm, his subsequent amputation, or his recent marriage to a wealthy widow that caused his lack of aggression.

Here is General Jackson's report of the battle:

In a few moments our entire line was engaged in a fierce and sanguinary struggle with the enemy.
As one Federal line was repulsed, another took its place and pressed forward as if determined by force of numbers and fury of assault to drive us from our positions.

Concerning the fury of this battle, here is the official battlefield report by the Federal Colonel Rufus Dawes who was involved in the fighting:

Our men on the left loaded and fired with the energy of madmen, and the men on the right worked with equal desperation. This stopped the rush of the Rebels and when they halted they fired upon us with deadly musketry. During a few awful moments, I could see by the lurid light of the powder flashes, the whole of both lines. The two lines were within fifty yards of each other pouring musketry into each other as fast as men could load and shoot.

Major Rufus Dawes, 6th Wisconsin

At noon, the fighting finally died down, more from exhaustion than tactics. While Jackson's men were cleaning their guns and caring for the wounded, the air was suddenly filled with cheering, for tramping down the dusty road leading to camp were the first men from Longstreet's division, late but at least finally there.[16]

This meeting of the Confederate "wings" virtually assured Pope's defeat as he now faced my entire force.[17]

---

[16] Another instant of tardiness by Longstreet caused even a bigger problem for Lee at Gettysburg.

[17] Confederate law prevented Lee from using brigades and divisions for

The next morning, August 30th, a confident Pope, thinking he had weakened General Jackson, again began to attack. The first he knew that Longstreet was on the field was when the right side of Jackson's Army, Longstreet's 25,000 strong in five divisions, counterattacked in a mass Confederate assault. In a short while the entire Federal left flank was utterly destroyed, and only the brilliant rear guard action by the brigade of one-armed, General Oliver Howard saved the rest of Pope's army.

The combat ended around 9 p.m. with the Union troops slowly retreating backwards, still firing, making their line at the edge of the woods. Other regiments also retired to the turnpike in an orderly fashion. I regret to say, despite the advantage we had in the number of troops, we did not do very well. The fight was essentially a draw, but at a heavy cost, with over 1,150 Union and 1,250 of my men either dead or wounded. The Stonewall brigade lost 340 out of 800. And I am a loss to

---

the Confederate Army as the Confederate Congress saved that right exclusively for the governors of the various Southern States. He therefore gave the name of "Wings" to two, and later three, corps.

reconcile the following: two Georgia regiments each lost more than a remarkable 70 percent of their troops. As General Jackson said, 'the fighting was fierce and bloody. On both sides, one out of every three men engaged in the fight was wounded or killed.'

During the second Battle of Bull Run, between the Rappahannock and Potomac Rivers, the Federals lost 14,462 men with more than 4,000 of them taken prisoner. In contrast, we lost just 9,474.

Lincoln, realizing he had made a serious mistake, recalled General McClellan to retake charge of the Federal Army. The Union men were happy and so was I.

Only three months before, the 100,000 strong Federal Army was at the gates of Richmond. I stopped McClellan there and then pushed him back all the way to the James River. I then reshaped the Confederate Army and assaulted the enemy, pushing them back to their own capitol, Washington.

Now that I had gained the momentum, I urged the Confederate Congress to let me take the war to the North. They agreed and soon we were on our way to Antietam Creek in Sharpsburg, Maryland.

We had had a serious bloodletting in Virginia and unfortunately for both armies, there was more to come.

(To McClellan) If we never try we shall never succeed

Abraham Lincoln

Chapter 15: The Battle of Antietam (Sharpsburg)

Headquarters Alexandria & Leesburg Road Near Dranesville, Virginia
September 3, 1862
Mr. President:
The present seems the most propitious time since the commencement of the war for the Confederate Army to enter Maryland. The two grand armies of the United States that have been operating in Virginia, though now united, are much weakened and demoralized. Their new levies, of which I understand sixty thousand

men have already been posted in Washington, are not yet organized, and will take some time to prepare for the field. If it is ever desired to give material aid to Maryland and afford her an opportunity of throwing off the oppression to which she is now subject, this would seem the most favorable. After the enemy had disappeared from the vicinity of Fairfax Court House and taken the road to Alexandria & Washington, I did not think it would be advantageous to follow him farther. I had no intention of attacking him in his fortifications, and am not prepared to invest them. (Even) If I had possessed the necessary munitions, I should be unable to supply provisions for the troops. I therefore determined while threatening the approaches to Washington, to draw the troops into Loudon, where forage and some provisions can be obtained, menace their possession of the Shenandoah Valley, and if I found practicable, to cross into Maryland.

The purpose, if discovered, will have the effect of carrying the enemy north of the Potomac, and if prevented, will not result in much evil. The army is not properly equipped for an invasion of an enemy's territory. It lacks much of the material for war, is feeble in transportation, the animals being much reduced, and the men are poorly provided with clothes, and in thousands of instances are destitute of shoes. Still we cannot afford to be idle, and though weaker than our opponents in men and military equipment, must endeavor to harass, if we cannot destroy them.

I am aware that the movement is attended with much risk, yet I do not consider success impossible, and shall endeavor to guard it from loss. As long as the army of the enemy are employed on this frontier I have no fears for the safety of Richmond, yet I earnestly recommend defense, by land and water, in the most perfect condition. A respectable force can be collected to defend its approaches by land, and the steamer Richmond I hope is now ready to clear the river of hostile vessels.

Should Genl [Braxton] Bragg find it impracticable to operate to advantage on his present frontier, his army, after leaving sufficient garrisons, could be advantageously employed in opposing the over-whelming numbers, which it seems to be the intention of the enemy now to concentrate in Virginia. I have already been told by prisoners that some of [General Don Carlos] Buell's cavalry have been joined to Genl Pope's army, and have reason to believe that the whole of McClellan's, the larger portions of Burnside's & Cox's and a portion of [General David] Hunter's, are united to a joint effort. What occasions me most concern is the fear of getting out of ammunition. I beg you will instruct the Ordnance Department to spare no pains in manufacturing a sufficient amount of the best kind, & to be particular in preparing that for the artillery, to provide three times as much of the long range ammunition as of that for smooth bore or short range guns. The points to which I desire the ammunition to be forwarded will be made known to the Department in time. If the Quartermaster Department can furnish any shoes, it would be the greatest relief to the unshod.

We have entered upon September, and the nights are becoming cool and some of the men have a need for

warmer clothes
I have the honor to be with high respect, your ob't servant,
R. E. Lee, General Commanding

As I intimated to the president in my letter, this seemed to me to be a propitious time to strike north. I would have liked to have gone directly to (assault) Washington, but their superior defenses, our lack of provisions and munitions, and the fact that they had a 2 to 1 numerical advantage in men gave me pause to reconsider an alternative target. For several reasons I chose Maryland. First it was my belief that the young men of Maryland would rise to the Confederate banner and join us. I remembered the Baltimore riots early in the war and knew there were many Marylanders among my troops. These were but a few of the many signs that the Marylanders were solid for the South and would back us up. To my dismay this did not happen.

Secondly I thought the people of Maryland, though they were a border state, would be more than happy to provision us with the bounty we saw in their farms and fields. This also did not happen. What did happen was I could count those who enlisted in our cause on the fingers of two hands.[18] And what provisions we obtained had to be bought and paid for. Truly in Maryland, we marched to Sharpsburg (Antietam) on empty bellies.

Little did I realize that this incursion north would result in a calamity of great significance. My greatest fear before the battle was running out of supplies and ammunition. But there was more than that at stake here. To my detriment, I did not foresee the profound political influence this battle would have on the war. Indeed, although we did not lose the battle, at best it could be considered a draw. When it was over we did leave the field. And when we left the field, it appeared that the Federals had won the day. President Lincoln then wisely chose that moment to declare the Emancipation Proclamation. When that proclamation became public, England and

---

[18] As a matter of fact, only 200 Maryland men joined up on the northern march. Even former Governor Enoch Lowe, an ardent Confederate sympathizer, failed to show up despite a telegram from General Lee asking him to do so.

France, who had been favorable to the South, immediately pulled back and no longer would support us. Of course, their reason was our investment in slavery.

Why do men fight who were born to be brothers?

James Longstreet

Chapter 16: Invasion of Maryland

I now had several options: I could draw back across the Rappahannock River and rest my exhausted and starving army. My army had been marching and fighting since June in the 'Seven Days Battles' near Richmond. Another option was to stay where we were. But I was now 100 miles from my supplies in Richmond and had no wagons to span the mileage and few mules to pull the imaginary wagons. By now the fields around us had been stripped of food to the discomfort of the farmers despite their loyalty to either side.

But I wanted to sustain my momentum and keep the initiative I had gained over McClellan and Pope. My greatest hope was if I could keep defeating the Yankees and give the Northern newspapers long lists of dead and wounded soldiers, they might sue for peace and leave us alone.

An invasion of Maryland looked like the best of all options. In Maryland, the fall harvest was coming in and that could at last feed my army properly. Also it would allow the Virginia farmers a bit of breathing room to gather in what remained of their crops without being harassed by starving soldiers. In addition, the invasion of Northern soil would surely bring the Union Army away from their haven in Washington and while following us, prevent them from again threatening Richmond at least until after winter. When both armies hunkered down for the winter I thought that breathing spell would give us the chance to find new ways to harass the enemy and perhaps even win the war. Also the Northern papers were full of the growth of opposition to the war. This opposition was being fueled by the Copperheads (a group of northerners against the war) led by the Ohio politician, Clement Vallandigham. An invasion up north with Confederate troops investing the Maryland countryside might electrify and put the fear of God into the anti-war Democrats in the upcoming November elections. In addition, reports from abroad indicated that England and France were looking with favor on the Confederate victories. A brazen invasion and even occupation in the heart of the North might induce those two world powers to recognize the Southern Confederacy and accord us diplomatic recognition. We had such great hopes of the European countries intervening, and since there was already talk of England intervening on our behalf it became a distinct possibility. But because of the Emancipation document the possibility of intervention died aborning.

****

This invasion of the north was a marked departure from President Davis' policy of fighting only defensively in the south but he finally gave his approval hoping this rude shock of invasion would induce Lincoln to let the errant sisters (states) go their own way.'

I gathered my army and we headed north. It was indeed a motley army that started off for Maryland. Fully one quarter of my men had no shoes. Their hats and uniforms, such as they were, were riddled with holes, and even the officers' clothing were in tatters. I was ashamed but at the same time extremely proud of these men. One other thing of note: although their personal hygiene was in question every man's rifle was clean and oiled and gleamed boldly in the morning sun.

But on the march, despite the excellent morale, we did have some problems. Because of the lack of shoes and severe hunger, many of the men started to straggle. Then another problem popped up. As we got closer to Maryland, some of the boys from North Carolina started to grumble. I asked the commander of their wing why they were complaining and was told, "They joined to fight to defend the South, not to invade the North."

Many of them, along with some Northern Virginia men, simply melted into the night and went home. But to their credit when we returned after the battle of Sharpsburg, there they were, ready to rejoin us again.

All-in-all, about 15,000 men dropped out on that march, but they were replaced by 20,000 troops sent by President Davis from Richmond.

Along with the straggle problem, I was plagued again by other disputes in the high command. General John Bell Hood was arrested by General Shank Evans for arguing over possession of some Federal wagons. These men were probably the two best brigadiers I had, so I quickly straightened them out when another dispute arose.

This time it was General A. P. Hill giving me cause for concern. It wasn't Longstreet, but General Jackson that got upset with him. It seems that Jackson was riding along the march urging the men to close up ranks when he saw Hill ignoring the stragglers trailing off and disappearing. A red-faced Jackson halted Hill's lead brigade and raced after Hill. Both men then got into a fierce confrontation that ended when Hill unbuckled his sword and handed it to Jackson. General Jackson refused the sword but placed Hill under arrest. Hill then got down off his horse and proceeded to the back of his last brigade and became the last man on the march. After a while, cooler heads prevailed and Hill once more took over his command.

After having to deal with generals behaving like children, I suffered another blow. While reading a map, a gust of wind took it right out of my hand and landed it over Traveller's eyes. The poor horse shied and then started to bolt. I grabbed for his bridle, but his temporary blindness drove him mad and he threw me to the ground. I wound up spraining both hands and breaking a bone in one of them. With splints on both hands I had to eschew riding my horse and instead rode in an ambulance.

Despite all these problems that affected my army, morale was high and you could see the steel in their eyes that said they were determined to overcome whatever enemy they faced. As one of my staff muttered when they marched by, "None but the heroes are left."

At the beginning of September, the army arrived at Leesburg, Virginia. There they were met by cheering crowds that embraced them and fed them. I even heard one old woman, with tears in her eyes shouting, "May the Lord bless your dirty, ragged souls."

Finally at White's Ford, with our band playing, *Maryland, My Maryland*, we crossed into the state of Maryland. The invasion of the North had begun. It was indeed a historic moment and a cavalry trooper standing next to me later said: "There were few moments, perhaps from the beginning to the close of the war, of excitement more intense, of exhilaration more delightful."

I was told later that as soon as we stepped into Maryland panic ensued in Washington. Like Paul Revere in the first revolution, Marylanders raced through Washington streets shouting, "The Rebels are coming!" There was even a steamer in the Washington Navy Yard waiting to take the Federal Cabinet and President to safety.

But instead of leaving, the president turned to the man he had recently replaced. He quickly named General McClellan, "Commander of the men and the fortifications defending Washington."

When questioned on that appointment, President Lincoln told his secretary, John Hay, "We must use the tools we have. If he can't fight himself, he excels in making others ready to fight." The words were providential for in a mere three days General McClellan had Pope's Army ready to march and spoiling for a fight. Late that afternoon, the Federal Army of Virginia left Washington to pursue us in Maryland.

Meanwhile, to insure cooperation from the population, I ordered strict regulation against pillaging. My men were to pay for anything they took. To their credit I heard of not one incident of theft or disorder by any of the men of my army.

I took time to inform the president of our progress:

Mr. President:
In Fredrick, Maryland, a Mr. Rosenstock took a picture of one of my divisions that was passing by his dry goods store.
A witness to the march said, "They were the dirtiest men I ever saw, a most ragged, lean and hungry set of wolves. Yet there was a dash about

them that the northern men lacked. [19]

We had dash all right, but we had problems, too. One wing commander, General Longstreet had a heel blister and was limping around his headquarters in carpet slippers. If that wasn't bad enough my other wing commander, General Jackson had been thrown earlier by a cantankerous horse, a gift from a Maryland farmer. Since that time, Jackson had been confined to his tent with a painful back ailment. His own horse, Little Sorrel had mysteriously disappeared and the patrol I sent out to find him was unsuccessful. And, since my hands were still in splints from my fall, it was fortunate for us that the Yankees didn't know about our infirmities or they would have attacked us for sure. The next night, however, Jackson felt well enough to go to church, the doctor lanced Longstreet's blister and I took a splint off one of my hands.

---

[19] The letter above was written by, General Lee to President Davis discussing the invasion of Maryland. Lee hoped to supplement his army by picking up volunteers in Maryland. He was sorely disappointed as most Marylanders ignored his entreaties. This letter was written twelve days prior to the Battle of Antietam.

Things were looking up. It's a good thing, too, for later that evening the Yankees attacked one of our outposts and General Stuart had to interrupt a ball he had organized to drive the Yankees off.

The next day I issued an official proclamation to gain men for our army and support for our cause:

TO THE PEOPLE OF MARYLAND

The army has come prepared to assist you with the power of its arms in regaining the rights of which you have been despoiled.

It is for you to decide your destiny, freely and without constraint.

This army will respect your choice whatever it may be.

GEN'L R.E. Lee
commanding

The proclamation was a waste of time. The answer came to me vividly when I saw most stores close their doors to us, and the ones that did stay open refused to take Confederate script. Seeing this refusal to help

I knew it was time to move on and ordered all our tents to be struck and the march toward Pennsylvania to begin again.

This was not just an exercise march as I had an important plan in mind. About a hundred miles north of where we were was a key bridge of the Pennsylvania Railroad line in the town of Harrison, Pennsylvania. Destruction of this bridge would sever an important Federal supply line between the east and west. After that we had our choice to invade, Philadelphia, Baltimore or even Washington.

But before we could think of invading one of those cities we would have to deal with the Federal troops at Harper's Ferry. I knew the place well, having been the commander that led to the capture of John Brown and his band of marauders when they had dreams of starting a slave insurrection beginning at Harper's Ferry.

The reason we had to now take Harper's Ferry was because that place stood on our supply route from the Shenandoah Valley. There were 12,000 Federals there that should have fled when we marched into Maryland but they did not, and now we had to deal with them.

McClellan still wanted to evacuate them, but the Federal high command would not allow it.

Now, to deal with this situation I had to split my army. First, I sent Longstreet into Pennsylvania toward Hagerstown. Next, I sent Generals Jackson, McLaws and Walker in pincer movements to surround Harper's Ferry and take the Federal strongpoint. After they had done so, they were then to march north, meet up with Longstreet and me for further orders.

All this activity of splitting the army into four units was spelled out in the famous, or should I say infamous, Order No. 191.

****

There is an ancient military axiom that states never to divide your army in the face of the enemy. I admit there is some risk in doing that, but there are times it can be of great benefit to do so. Because of the danger of such a document falling into enemy hands and allowing the enemy to get between the pieces of the divided army, the commanders receiving such an order will usually take great care in disposing of it after reading it. For instance when General Longstreet committed the order to memory he chewed the paper until it was pulp and then spit it into a fire.

The problem started when Jackson read his copy and then made another copy of it and sent the new copy to General Hill. Neither Generals Jackson nor Hill were aware that there was an official copy of my order that I sent directly to General Hill. Somehow MY order was never given to General Hill and we later surmised that one of his staff officers may have thought it of little importance, wrapped it around some cigars and promptly lost it in the Confederate camp area.

Longstreet raised an objection to my dividing the army into fours but the Northern newspapers were full of information that said McClellan was again the Yankee Commander and I was counting on his excess caution in not attacking us while we were vulnerable. I told my staff, 'He is an able general but an exceedingly cautious one.'

Meanwhile Jeb Stuart's troopers were leaving false stories about our army being 100,000 strong and McClellan's own intelligence telling him it was 200,000. This was wonderful for us, as we only had 60,000 men. These excessive numbers confused McClellan and slowed him even further.

Suddenly God deserted us and the fortunes of war turned against us. It was Saturday the 27th of September 1862, a date that will live in infamy. It was on that day that the order 191 was found, not by a Confederate soldier, but by two Yankees. After the war, those two soldiers told me what happened. One of them, Sergeant Bloss was lying on the ground resting when he saw something in the grass. The other man, his friend, Corporal Mitchell, saw it at the same time and they laughingly scrambled for it. Mitchell got to it first and quickly opened it. To the corporal's amazement, there were three cigars wrapped in a sheet of paper. While Corporal Mitchell lit one of the cigars, Sergeant Bloss took the sheet from his friend and read it. It was addressed to General Hill and the heading read:

"Special order No. 191"

It was the plan of operation for the Confederate Army. Of course the two Federal veteran non-coms immediately delivered the order to their company commander who sent it up the chain of command to General McClellan. The General was just dismounting from his horse, *Dan Webster*, when he was handed the paper. When McClellan read the order, he thought it was too good to be true. He asked for someone who might know the men on my staff. Luckily for him, General Pittman was available and he knew my adjutant's handwriting. He immediately confirmed it.

"Now I've got them," McClellan exclaimed. "Now I know what to do."

General McClellan immediately put his troops in motion toward the mountain gaps. If they got through the mountain gaps they would be in the middle of the four pieces of my army. It was McClellan's chance to destroy us one piece at a time.

Thank god for Confederate ingenuity at the vulnerable gaps, knowing Longstreet's troops were on the way, but still hours away, General D. H. Hill, the commander at one of the major gaps devised a ruse to delay the Federals at his front. He got all his non-combatants, cooks, staff officers, teamsters and even wounded men, and lined them up facing the game, but tired troops of General Cox. It worked! General Cox rested his worn troops and asked McClellan for reinforcements.

Controlling this gap was so important to us that, hand splints and all, I mounted Traveller and went to Fox's Gap myself. Almost as soon as I got there, here came Hood's division. As they filed by me, I could tell they were agitated. I thought they were fidgety about going into battle, but that was not the case. Suddenly the men filing past me began to shout, 'Give us Hood, we want Hood.'

I raised my hat and answered, 'You shall have him, gentlemen.' I realized he was still under arrest for insubordination and thought I could easily fix that. Not so.

I sent for Hood and told him if he expressed remorse he could once more lead his men. To my amazement, he refused my offer and started to argue with me. I shook my head and interrupted him. "General Hood, I will suspend your arrest until the impending battle is decided." That did it. Hood rode to the front of his division and together they charged toward Fox's Gap.

In the long run, sending Hood up there and Longstreet later wasn't enough. When Taylor gave me the reports of the battles that night, all I could say to him was, “We cannot afford this disparity of casualties.” Of the 18,000 men I had in the gaps, we had lost 2,700 including 800 missing. The Federals had sent in more men but only lost 1,800.’ I sent word to McLaws saying, “The day has gone against us. Abandon Harper’s Ferry and join us in Virginia.”

By ten o’clock that night I was tired. I was tired of the splints on my hands, I was tired of no sleep, I was tired of losing so many men to Yankee guns, and I was tired of being so far north. Then Major Taylor handed me General Jackson’s battle report and suddenly I wasn’t a bit tired anymore. It appears that our actions in the gaps gave Jackson time to tighten his grip on Harper’s Ferry.

And tighten he did. The three Generals, Jackson, Walker and Hill, finally took Harper’s Ferry and captured the entire garrison except General Benjamin Davis’ cavalry that had made a daring escape against great odds. I daresay General Davis’ Mississippi accent helped him greatly in the escape and the capture of 40 Confederate ordnance wagons.[20] And he lost not a single man. When I heard about Davis' exploit, I wanted to give him a medal, too.

Alas there was no rest for Jackson, or his foot cavalry, as I needed them in Sharpsburg as fast as they could get to me.

I read later that a captured Yankee trooper watching Jackson's men hurrying to me wrote:

They were silent as ghosts; ruthless and rushing in their speed; ragged, earth-colored, disheveled and devilish, as though keen on the scent of hot blood. The shuffle of their badly shod feet on the hard surface of the pike was so rapid as to be continuous like the hiss of a great serpent.

On the morning of September 15th, my army and I crossed the meandering creek

---

[20] He was actually stopped by a Confederate patrol during the escape and the Mississippi drawl he had fooled the Rebel Soldiers so badly they actually helped him by guiding him down the right path to freedom.

called the Antietam and headed toward Sharpsburg.

The men were weary and footsore from the long march from South Mountain, so after a climb of a half a mile or so on a slope in front of the town, I called a halt and let the men take a rest. While they rested I poured over the map of the area and then looked at the surrounding terrain. Just in front of the town of Sharpsburg was a ridge that overlooked all of the approaches. I turned to Major Taylor and said with finality, "We will make our stand on that ridge." Just then a courier from Jackson came up and with a leap from his sweating horse landed just in front of me. The courier saluted. "General Lee," he said in an excited voice, "it is my great pleasure to announce to you that General Jackson has captured Harper's Ferry with hundreds if not thousands of stands of weapons."

I saluted the courier and turned to Major Taylor. "That's great news that will surely cheer the men. Detail some officers to announce the news to all the troops and then tell the men we have to get ready to move up and dig in on that ridge ahead."

I turned back to the courier and told him to wait a minute. I began to write a note to Jackson to tell him I needed him. He was to leave a detail at Harper's Ferry, and he and his men to hurry to Sharpsburg as soon as possible. After writing the note I gave it to the courier, saluted and told him to get back to General Jackson as fast as he could.

My problem now was that I had only 18,000 men at hand and Jackson was 12 miles away. The Federals, under McClellan were 60,000 strong.

But I had an ally and that ally was McClellan himself. As I told a member of my staff, I knew that he would delay attacking for at least a day or two.[21]

I next climbed the ridge and examined the ground. Pleased at my selection, I then deployed my men in a four-mile long line on the ridge that was anchored on the Potomac River. The terrain was mostly in our favor as there was an open field of fire on almost all of the ground facing us. In addition, there were

---

[21] Lee was exactly right, as the first Federals to attack Lee's troops was Hooker's First Corps on September 17th.

stone fences for my men to hide behind and rail fences for the Yankees to get over. There was even a sunken road for the men to use as a natural trench. Best of all, just next to the ridge was a good road that would allow me to shift men back and forth without hindrance.

There was only one feature of the terrain that troubled me and that was the Potomac River. That river was at our back and left little room to maneuver if we had to fall back. Even worse there was only one place my troops could cross the Potomac and that was Boteler's Ford. If my troops were forced back into that bottleneck they might face an Armageddon from the accurate Federal artillery.

For a few anxious minutes, I tossed the decision back and forth in my mind. At length, I decided: I will dig in right here and only Heaven and God will move me.

I learned later that after his army arrived, McClellan showed up in high spirits. Even though he failed to save Harper's Ferry he had been victorious at South Mountain.

After he notified Washington of his "Glorious Victory", he received the following wire from the Federal President: "God bless you and all with you. Destroy the rebel army if possible."

But instead of trying to destroy us, General McClellan and his army acted like they were getting ready for a grand parade instead of a grand battle.

Here we were, outnumbered, outgunned and with our backs up against the Potomac and the Federals were watching a horse race. Yes, two Federal men on horseback were racing across fields in front of our lines and instead of shooting them our men cheered them on. In short order I got our officers to stop the cheering and got the men hunkered down ready for battle.

The next morning, after marching all night, Jackson's men arrived at Sharpsburg footsore and weary, but ready to fight.

As he did several times during the "Seven Days", McClellan repeated his usual caution and restraint. Instead of assaulting us when we were most vulnerable, with our backs against a river, McClellan waited a full 24 hours before he got his army ready. That evening, General Hooker moved his corps and got into a mean fight with John Bell Hood and his Texans. The coming of night ended the battle and then a cold rain descended on us.

At 5:30 the next morning, Hooker's First corps began their advance against Colonel James Walker of Stonewall Jackson's corps. During a huge artillery bombardment from both sides, Walker was subsequently wounded and had to leave the field.[22] His men put up such a spirited defense that they soon had Hooker's Pennsylvanians retreating backward.

Both sides fed men in haphazardly and soon the entire four miles was ablaze with rifle and cannon fire. Soon there was a massive attack by a Wisconsin brigade that tore a hole in Jackson's line. Only a magnificent charge by Hood's Texans plugged the gap and stabilized the line. For a short while the guns fell silent while both armies licked their wounds. The battle had raged for almost four hours and this was just the beginning.

---

[22] Colonel Walker was a student of Jackson's at VMI in 1852. Jackson accused Walker of talking in class. Discipline was strict at VMI and this accusation led to Walker being expelled. After the dismissal the enraged student challenged his professor to a duel. Cooler heads prevailed and the duel was never held.

During this battle of cannons and wills, I was just in back of my line of men loading and firing at the Federals. McClellan, in direct contrast, was a mile away from the battle at his headquarters tent.

In the midst of the fighting, I found myself catching stragglers and ordering them back into the fight.[23]

Meanwhile both armies got into a fierce fight at a place called the East and West Woods. For five hours, McLaws and Sumner stood toe to toe exchanging fire in the killing field.

In the center, our General Rhodes found the Sunken Road and lined up his men there. It was a perfect defensive position and in a short while, its name was changed to Bloody Lane. Even the vaunted Irish Brigade could not dent the position held by Rhodes. Finally the Yankees found a weak spot and together with a stupendous error by one of my officers,

---

[23] In one incident Lee intercepted a straggler carrying a pig. Lee, totally enraged, called a sergeant who arrested the straggler, pig and all. Lee sent the errant soldier, under guard, to General Jackson to be shot. Instead of shooting the hapless boy, Jackson put him in the hottest part of the battle where he fought like a tiger and redeemed himself. After the battle his captain said, "He lost his pig, but saved his bacon."

charged into the Sunken Road. The Yankees took the road and routed the retreating Confederate soldiers.[24]

****

There was no respite for either side, for as the fighting subsided at the Sunken Road it flared up at what is now known as Burnside's Bridge. It was here that my plan was so vulnerable, as General Toombs had only 550 men and faced Burnsides army of 11,000. But Toombs had a marked advantage. His troops were embedded in a 100 foot wooded bluff overlooking the bridge. Toombs also had 12 pieces of artillery behind him, zeroed in on the bridge.

At 10 a.m., with General McClellan urging Burnside on, the Federals attacked the bridge. For three hours my men held off attack after attack until 1 p.m. Then, running low on

---

[24] The wounded General Rhodes ordered a "Wheel right" to counter a Federal charge, but his lieutenant colonel got the order wrong and ordered a retreat. The Charging Federals then took over the Sunken Road and captured 300 Confederates to boot. Only two Rebel officers, Hill and Colquitt went unscathed. Future Governor of Georgia, John B. Gordon was wounded five times. Confederate General Anderson was mortally wounded, as was the Federal General, Israel Richardson.

ammunition and with a large Federal force surrounding them, they made a skillful withdrawal, moving to a prearranged position a half-mile back. In the battle for the bridge the total casualties for the Union was 500, including several Union generals, while for Toombs and his small army the casualty count was 160, but that day the South also lost several generals.

Now that the Union IX Corps had taken the bridge, and even with 20 percent losses, Burnside was in a position to destroying my army. Knowing this, I had sent for A. P. Hill and his men to come to the Confederate rescue. He left Harper's Ferry and cut cross-country, marching 17 miles in eight hours. He got there just in time to support Toombs and save my army. Soon Burnside, because of his losses on the day, pulled his men all the way back to the heights above the bridge. He and McClellan had us defeated but they couldn't see it. Truly, Burnside and McClellan snatched defeat from victory. Federal caution had saved my army at Sharpsburg.

After 12 hours of continued slaughter, the guns finally fell silent on the heights above Burnside's Bridge.

An aide of General Jackson riding where the thick of the battle had been fought wrote later:

The dead and dying lay over it (the field) as (thick as) harvest sheaves... As we walked through the field my horse trembled under me in terror.

The final casualty count for the Federals was 12,410. For my army it was 10,316. The worst thing was the Federals could replace their portion of the 22,726 casualties. We could not.[25]

****

The next day both armies lay hunkered down at the front eyeing each other warily. An informal truce was declared and units from both sides began to treat the wounded and bury the dead.

---

[25] For all intents and purposes, on September 18, 1862 the battle was over. When all the casualties were counted it would stand as the highest single day of mayhem of any American war. Also, the casualty count was vastly undercounted, as many of the wounded would soon succumb to their injuries.

I was personally astounded at the carnage and knowing McClellan's aversion to blood, I thought he would be loath to continue the struggle. Going to the rear gave no relief from the butchery as one then came on the surgeon's tents and their piles, some rising several feet, of amputated arms and legs.[26]

For a while, I contemplated turning the Federal right but due to my overwhelming losses I soon thought better of it and began to think only of getting my army back to safer territory. Besides McClellan was getting fresh troops while we had none. Also we still had to cross the bridge at Boteler's Ford and risk the Federal artillery, but I felt McClellan had had enough and I was right. He did not follow us. However, he did have second thoughts the next morning and sent his cavalry after us. They were too late and arrived at Boteler's Ford just as the last of my army had crossed over into Virginia.

---

[26] With one in four men a casualty, one would wonder what had been gained for either side. But since after this battle Lee left the field and retreated back to Virginia, President Lincoln treated Antietam as a victory and felt secure in releasing the Emancipation Proclamation. This changed forever the reason for all the casualties and made England and France shy away from recognizing the slave holding South.

Except for a mauling of the 118th Pennsylvania Regiment, who were following A. P. Hill's retreating troops, the battle of Antietam was over.

George McClellan

I could always count on him to take his time

Mr. President, the Emancipation Proclamation will be like the last shriek!

William Seward

Chapter 17: The Battle of Fredericksburg

Even though the battle of Antietam was technically a draw, my army did ultimately leave the field, so for all intents and purposes the battle was a strategic victory for the Union. Even though it was a suspect victory for the Union, it was enough for President Lincoln to release the Emancipation Proclamation to the world. In my opinion, he would have NOT released that document if it were a Union defeat.

But no leader of a nation, if he had been victorious, would cashier the head of his army. And that is just what Lincoln did. By the battle reports of McClellan's subordinates

Lincoln must have surmised that my army was on our last legs. According to their reports it was clear they had urged McClellan to assault us, but instead of attacking us with his 2 to 1 advantage, McClellan invoked his usual "caution" and let us get away unscathed.

My guess is that Lincoln fired his commander because he was fed up with McClellan's excuses. He wanted a man like Grant, who would fight like a bulldog and once he got his teeth in you, would never let go.

****

In the information I asked for at the beginning of this narrative, I was told by one of the Federal staff that on November 7th 1862, General Burnside was a visitor to General McClellan's tent relieving him of command and taking over the 120,000 man Federal Army.

Unlike McClellan, Burnside did not hesitate, and in just two days he ordered a 40-mile lightning dash cross-country to Fredericksburg. It was clear the taking of Fredericksburg would give General Burnside a direct highway for the Army of the Potomac to capture Richmond.

This change of command must have inspired the Federal Army for in just two days of marching, the lead elements of the Army of the Potomac was on Stafford Heights overlooking the Rappahannock River at the gates of Fredericksburg.

This was one time that I did not anticipate the Federals coming to Fredericksburg nor the speed of the Union forces on the march. This left the Army of Northern Virginia at a serious disadvantage. What I had done that put us in jeopardy was sending one wing of my army under Stonewall Jackson to the Shenandoah Valley and another wing, commanded by General Longstreet, to confront the Yankees at Culpepper.

What saved us was that Burnside could not get at my depleted army without crossing the Rappahannock River.

Because all of the bridges spanning the Rappahannock had been demolished, Burnside lost no time in notifying Washington that he needed pontoon equipment to have his army cross the river to reach Fredericksburg.

Since the beginning of this rebellion, the Federal Command always seemed to have a cog missing in their fighting machine. During a battle, a vital order was mislaid or not delivered. Supplies that were requested would not be transported, or would be sent to the wrong place. Brigades would be given the wrong order and would move leaving a gap in the line that the Rebels would quickly exploit. All this would cost the Union men fighting the battle numerous casualties.

Inefficient Federal bureaucracy, military miscommunication, and in this case, heavy rains delayed the arrival of the pontoon bridges until the 25th of November, 8 days after they were requested. God had answered my prayers, as just as the pontoons arrived, so did the rest of my Army.[27]

After command discussions on where to put the bridges, the Federals got busy, and in the darkness, began to put together the bridges. When two of them were almost completed I ordered Barksdale to get into the Fredericksburg streets, and ask the owners to let his men into their houses next to the river to stop the completion of the bridges.

---

[27] Even the measurements of the bridges were wrong for the river.

When he got ready, Barksdale's Mississippians let fly a barrage of Minié balls that took such a toll of the Union engineers the completion of the bridges ceased. Nine times the engineers tried to complete the bridges and nine times they failed.

Realizing he couldn't get at Barksdale's men with his infantry, Burnside called upon his artillery chief, Brigadier General Hunt to do the job. Hunt lined up 150 guns on Stafford Heights and at mid-day let loose a barrage of shot and shell at every house and corner of Fredericksburg and its environs.

The bombardment lasted for two hours and wreaked havoc on the town. When it was over, the engineers again approached the bridges to complete the crossing when inexplicably, even bizarrely, rifle fire began again, this time coming from the rubble left by the cannons, causing more engineers to fall into the freezing Rappahannock River either dead or wounded.

At wits end, Burnside asked for volunteers to get into scows and row the 400 feet across to the other bank and root out the riflemen stopping the Federal army progress.

There is nothing like the heart of a volunteer and very soon the volunteers were across the river and charging at the Mississippians. I realized my boys had no experience in street fighting, and that they were confused. I gave the order to Barksdale to have his men fall back. With tears in my eyes, I watched them bravely ignore my orders and contest each cobble-strewn street until dusk brought an end to the fighting.

With the last of the daylight I saw the engineers complete the bridges and the Federals move over them and occupy the town.

The next morning dawned cold and hazy. Slowly at first then more quickly more Union soldiers poured into the town of Fredericksburg unopposed. Instead of organizing themselves to attack us, the Federals changed from soldiers to pirates. To my chagrin and amazement they spent the better part of the day and into the evening looting and vandalizing the shops and homes.

A Connecticut minister whom I met later, sent me this graphic account of their shameful behavior:

I saw men break down the doors to fine houses, enter and with axes shatter mirrors, lamps and even watched them destroy a fine grand piano...

I do thank the minister for sending me this information but it is an incident I no longer wish to speak of or even think of. Now that we are one nation again we must put those most unpleasant episodes behind us and look forward to increased friendship.

By now I had Jackson on my left and Longstreet on my right. We looked down on the destruction of the Town of Fredericksburg from the hills called Marye's Heights.

The Georgians under Cobb had a sunken road, much like the one at Antietam, and stone retaining walls along Telegraph Road (the main road to Richmond). This formed a natural ready-made trench that gave Cobb's men an open field of fire and good concealment. To assist Cobb, Old Pete, as his men called Longstreet, had put his considerable artillery along Marye's Heights protected by his five divisions of Veteran Confederates.

My entire line of defense stretched seven miles and was designed to have interlocking fire along the entire front. I daresay that not even a swift chicken could climb the heights without getting plucked by my gunfire. But to my everlasting regret, Burnside chose to try!

Jackson's troops were on more level ground so those people chose to try him first. To compensate for the weaker position, Jackson positioned his four divisions one behind the other for a mile deep. Even then the Yankees would have to get past the deadly Longstreet Artillery crossfire before they got to Jackson's infantry waiting for them.

On December 13, the assault began. First Franklin's Division went against Jackson, While Sumner's men waited to scale Marye's Heights.

Franklin, much like his former commander McClellan, was a cautious man, but this was no time for caution. His men, led by Meade, were cut to ribbons first with artillery and then by Jackson's musketry. But unfortunately for us, Jackson had left a serious gap in his defensive line and the competent Meade found and exploited it. His men gained the crest of the hill but met up with a scratch Confederate force led by General Maxcy Gregg who stopped them.

Gregg lost his life, but Jackson saw the gap and quickly sent in his reserve, drove the Federals back and plugged the hole. Jackson then counter-attacked but was stopped by the Federal Artillery.

Impatient at the fighting at Jackson's front, Sumner began his attack on Marye's Heights. The Union soldiers had to run across a water-filled ditch then move through an open 400-yard stretch of ground just to reach the base of Marye's Heights. Their goal was the stone wall at the top of the heights shielding the Confederate infantry. Longstreet's artillery was just waiting there for the Federals to start up the heights. As I said before, a chicken could not survive on that field when the artillery opened on it. In one hour, the Federals lost 3,000 men, but the insanity continued.

Despite the three divisions Burnside then hurled at us, my Confederates held fast. From my perch on Telegraph Hill, I watched the carnage with tears in my eyes. *So much bravery and so much death*, I thought. General Longstreet was beside me and I turned to him and expressed my grief. "It is well that war is so terrible," I said, "lest we should grow too fond of it."

Wave after wave of bluecoats were ordered up the heights, but not one man got near the stone wall. Finally, part of one brigade got to within 25 yards of the wall then fell apart when they were scythed down by our muskets.

Finally, darkness fell and the bloodshed stopped. Then the terrible cries of the wounded and dying started and lasted through the night. The screams and shrieks were so unnerving that men from both sides ignored their officer's orders and treated the wounded.

That night, Major Taylor brought me the casualty list. We had lost 5,300 men while Burnside had thrown 12,600 into the cauldron of war.

The next day Burnside wrote orders for another charge, but cooler heads prevailed preventing any more suicide.

It was a victory, but a hollow one for us. How and where would I replace the 5,300 men I lost? Those people would easily replace their losses, but not only could I not replace the men, but where would I get the supplies we expended in the battle. It was a puzzle I had to solve.

****

It was ten days until Christmas, and the Yankees were gone. The snows will come soon and the killing that was sure to follow Fredericksburg would be postponed until the Spring. Or so I thought.

Stonewall Jackson

Who could not conquer with such troops as these?

Jackson has lost his left arm but I have lost my right.

Robert E. Lee

Chapter 18: Chancellorsville

I was wrong about Burnside leaving and going into winter quarters after the butchery at Fredericksburg. For the rest of December and most of January, he and his army stayed in place across the Rappahannock just opposite us. It was hard to believe, but in late January, once again Burnside decided to attack.

I have since learned, Burnside and his scouts studied all along the Rappahannock for a place to assault us. But everywhere he went I had the men make a big show of digging in and covering the open ground under the heights with interlocking fire from both muskets and artillery. Shifting men back and forth, I was able to cover 25 miles of defensive line.

After losing so many men in futile suicide charges, Burnside grieved his mistake of direct assault and following deep thought and consultation with his officers he decided on moving against us with deception. He determined to move 10 miles from Fredericksburg to United States Ford, cross the Rappahannock there, and then move toward Marye's Heights. This sweeping maneuver would put him directly on the flank of my army. It was a brilliant plan and had I been completely aware of it I would have been very concerned.

His total plan was as follows: one division would prepare to cross the Rappahannock and charge Marye's Heights just as they had done before. The men would bring up siege guns, the cavalry would ride back and forth and the infantry would behave as if they would again charge up into our guns. This would keep us busy while Burnside, behind this elaborate feint, quietly began to move his two remaining divisions away.

Part of Burnsides written order said;

The great and auspicious moment has arrived to strike a great and mortal blow to the rebellion, and to gain that decisive victory which is due the country.

As I said before the plan was brilliant but sometimes in the affairs of men the Lord takes a hand in things and strategies go awry. That night, as the two Union Divisions began to haul their guns and bridges down the road, the heavens opened up and a deluge of biblical proportions fell on the men, the horses, the guns and the bridges. By the next morning all of the men and equipment of the two Federal Divisions were floating on a sea of mud. Three and four horses were attached to guns and bridges to no avail. Men's shoes stuck in the mud and in many cases were sucked off the feet of Union soldiers trying to march in the muck and mire the roads had become.

After a while Burnside stood, as soaking wet as any private, and watched the debacle before him, his hopes of redeeming the prestige he lost at Fredericksburg departing in a sea of muck!

I was told that after reading the Fredericksburg battle reports at the War Department, Lincoln put his head in his hands and sat still for a long while. Some even said they saw tears falling from his sad face. When he was informed of the "Mud March" he was galvanized into action.

Lincoln immediately called for a meeting with his cabinet to name a new commander. But he was too late, as before the meeting started, a letter of resignation from Burnside arrived.

****

Lincoln's choice for the new commander for the Army of the Potomac was the dapper and energetic, Joseph Hooker. I was told soon after I asked for information from my former opponents that General Hooker was not a surprise for the job of commander as he apparently had been aiming for the job all along. In fact some said he had been carping about the army leadership to Washington even before and after recent battles. (He even had a private audience with President Lincoln where he denigrated the Federal Army command.)

In any event I must say that, despite his reputation as a drinker and carouser, when he took command, Hooker's energy and discipline got the Union Army into excellent military shape. So much so that by late April, when the roads hardened, he was again marching his men to battle.

Although I hate to admit it when he made his move against me it was unexpected and excellent. Hooker swung his army around us far to the left and on the last evening in April closed in on Chancellorsville towards our rear.

Once again circumstances or God intervened and saved us. Like the fox in the Negro story of "Tar Baby", Hooker marched into an extension of the thickets in the "Wilderness" around Chancellorsville and got stuck there. At least stuck long enough for me to wake up to the danger and get my scattered army consolidated. But before I could get my army entirely together to confront him, his courage failed and instead of getting out of the woods to attack, he stayed put in the thickets and allowed us to trap him there.

Instead of being satisfied with both armies at a standoff, I ordered Jackson to meet me to discuss a plan I had in mind. The plan I thought of would be no less than the final destruction the Federal Army and then maybe we could get Washington to sue for peace.

Little did I know that this would be the last collaboration between me, and my right arm!

That night before a small fire, General Jackson and I sat on two old cracker boxes and conversed. While drawing lines in the dirt, I outlined my plan to Jackson. Instead of questioning or arguing the points, as Longstreet would have,[28] a small smile lit up Jackson's face when he heard my plan, and he nodded his agreement at every point. When I finished I asked if he had anything to add. Still smiling he stood up, took my hand and simply said, "I must go now and get my men

---

[28] Twice, once at second Manassas and again at Gettysburg, Lee listened to Longstreet to the detriment of his plan. In fact the kernels of much of the tragedy at Gettysburg were sown at the moment Lee yielded to Longstreet at Manassas, and Longstreet became aware that he would.

ready to execute the most audacious and brilliant strategy of the war."

The plan we had agreed on was the following: we would divide our army in two. Jackson would take 30,000 men and cross in front of Hooker (this was the most dangerous part) and go around to his rear. While Jackson did the envelopment, I would take the balance of 15,000 men and hold off Hooker's 90,000 men with feints and small attacks by my skirmishers.

On May 2, 1863, Jackson and his men began their precarious circuit around Hooker to his rear.

It's not as if Hooker was totally blind to what was happening. Jackson's men were not completely silent and several times Federal headquarters were notified of Confederate troop movements. But Hooker had a case of the McClellan "slows" and did not react.

Why those people did not respond to the reports of Confederate troop movements is still a mystery to me. One would have to ask the Federal command why they didn't they wake up!.

At 5 p.m. Jackson was in place behind a confused Hooker. His men were ready to charge but Jackson would not let them go just yet. He waited five, ten, fifteen minutes, until his men were so excited they were like a steel spring, wound up and ready to shoot forward. After a few more minutes Jackson then yelled "GO", unleashing his 30,000 howling Rebels in an overwhelming attack on Hooker's rear and right flank.

In the Rebels way were the Immigrant Germans of the Federal Eleventh Corps. After shattering them, the Confederates pushed the entire Union Army, at the time was getting ready for supper, a full two miles before they could recover and stop the now exhausted Confederates.

That was not good enough for Jackson. "Let the men rest for a few moments then we will continue," he said to his staff. "We will reconnoiter the Yanks and then drive them to perdition."

At 8 p.m. Jackson went to the front line with his staff and scouted the hastily constructed Federal line. He found the gaps and turned back to galvanize his troops for a final victory.

While returning to his men, a nervous unit of North Carolinian skirmishers mistakenly shot at the returning staff command and JACKSON FELL MORTALLY WOUNDED.

The long marches in the heat and rain, the immense risk of dividing our army in the face of the enemy, and the clandestine strategy between General Jackson and myself, and then the unfortunate death of my trusted subordinate, led to no less than a slugging match on three places in the Chancellorsville patch of Hell.

During the battle on May 3rd, Hooker continued to act timidly. Instead of using the untapped reservoir of his army, he abandoned key positions to me. Soon we were pushing the Federals back relentlessly. Hooker was like a punch drunk fighter on his heels always backing up.

One of our bombs, I was told, struck a post Hooker was leaning against and he fell unconscious for a half hour. During that time several Federal Commanders began to exert the untapped might of the Federal Army. But they did not have enough time to put their plans in effect as Hooker woke in time to cancel them and continue his ineffective restraint. The restraint worked, but it worked for us. By mid-morning our infantry smashed through the final Federal resistance and met in the center clearing of Chancellorsville.

Just as we were celebrating the victory word came to me that another Federal Unit had broken through and threatened our rear. I immediately led a portion of my army toward the sound of the guns.[29] After a short while that battle was over. On the 4th, I then returned to Chancellorsville to be present at the finish of Hooker.

Unfortunately, when I got ready, he had re-crossed the Rappahannock and left the area.

The campaign by General Hooker was wonderfully conceived but poorly executed. The battle of Chancellorsville cost the Union 14,000 casualties. We lost 10,000. But as I said before they could replace their losses, we could not.

Of all the 24,000 casualties on both sides none would be more missed than Jackson.

---

[29] The May 3rd battle mentioned here was The Battle of Salem Church and was another Confederate victory.

Just the thought of losing him brought tears to my eyes. They still do.

He was the one commander I could absolutely trust to do what I asked, but now he was gone. I remembered thinking at the time; *the Confederacy rested half on his shoulders. Now that weight is all on mine.*

****

To the Honorable Jefferson Davis
The Confederate White House
Richmond Virginia
By telegram May 7, 1863
Mr. President:
The conduct of our troops at Chancellorsville cannot be too highly praised. Attacking largely superior numbers in strongly entrenched positions, their heroic courage overcame every obstacle of nature and art, and achieved triumph most honorable to our arms.
With all their loss, our loss was greater as I regret to say that the noble

General and dear friend, Thomas Jackson was mortally wounded. Could I have directed events, I would have chosen for the good of the country to have been disabled in his stead.
His men, his subordinates and especially myself will miss him greatly.
Respectfully, your obedient servant,
Gen'l R. E. Lee

****

In addition, I wrote the following to my wife:

To Mary Lee
Richmond ,Virginia

My dear Mary:
Bryan[30] *arrived yesterday with your letters. The one to Charlotte with the Churchman will go by the first courier in that direction, indeed it has*

30 Lee's mess steward

already gone.

It would give me great pleasure to go to Richmond that I might see you even for a little while, & I must try and do so before you leave, but I cannot now say when.

I am glad to hear of so many weddings. The young people have a great deal to do in the present exhausted state of the country.

Now I have some sad news to tell you. Although the battle of Chancellorsville was a resounding Confederate victory, I have lost my right arm — General Thomas Jackson is dead. He was a great general and a great man. I know every time he was near Richmond and not on duty he would love to visit with you and share his love of Christ with you and the girls.

I know you will miss him and I already miss him terribly. But as always we must trust the Lord and try

to understand His wishes.
Give my love to everybody & believe me always yours.
Robert
P.S. I get the Churchman newspaper regularly now. Have you paid the subscription? If you have not, let me know and I will pay for it myself.

Gettysburg was the high water mark of the Confederacy

General John B. Gordon

Chapter 19: Gettysburg

The First Day, July 1, 1863

The battle of Gettysburg began, not with a musket shooting or a cannon blasting, but with a meeting of five old men. You see, young men go into the cauldron of fire and brimstone, but it is we old men who send them there.

Although the elements of surprise and envelopment decidedly won us the battle of Chancellorsville, we gained nothing more than a reprieve from the relentless pressure of the Federal Armies and their 'On to Richmond strategy.'

President Davis and the five members of his cabinet met with me on May 14, 1863. I started the meeting by telling them, the circumstances that made me march into Maryland and get into the bloodletting at Antietam had not changed. Nine months after the Maryland invasion, we were back where we started.

The situation of my army was this: the South was partially occupied by Federal Forces. In addition I had little forage for my cavalry. Also it distressed me no end that after fighting and winning battle after battle my army was still hungry,[31] poorly clothed and most of my men had no shoes.

The meeting was held in an atmosphere of deep gloom. Jackson had just been buried in Lexington near his precious VMI; Grant was threatening Vicksburg, and in the east, the opposing armies were deadlocked.

I then proposed my plan. "What we face," I said, "was an either/or situation. Either we retreat to Richmond and try to stand up to a siege that was then sure to come, or we invade Pennsylvania and relieve the problems of food and forage." As I spoke about the invasion,

---

[31] Lee told General Henry Heth, "The question of food for this army gives me more trouble and uneasiness than anything else. After all, can you ask a man to fight on and on with an empty belly?"

President Davis shook his head negatively while the rest of the cabinet looked horrified.

But I was not finished. While ignoring their reactions I then began to explain my reasoning. "A successful invasion," I said, "might induce Britain and France to intervene on behalf of the South. Also with conditions as they are now, I cannot feed and clothe my army. And in Pennsylvania, my men will find plenty of food while keeping the Yankees busy, and will give the farmers of Virginia time to plant and reap a decent harvest. In addition, an invasion of the North would encourage the copperheads and peace agitators to demand an end to the war and let the South go her own way. It will also encourage the Peace Democrats in the Northern Congress to stand up and demand a finish to the killing and destruction."

For three days, I stood before the cabinet and had to argue and hammer home my points until finally it came down to a vote. Despite General Regan's last minute histrionics about forgetting Pennsylvania and going to the relief of Pemberton at Vicksburg, the cabinet and President voted 5 to 1 in favor of the Pennsylvania invasion.

Now there was a lot to do so instead of going home to my family, I hurried back to the army to begin some vital reorganization.

Before Jackson's death I had two corps, one led by Jackson and the other by my old warhorse, "Pete", as his men call him, Longstreet. The number of men in each corps was approximately 30,000. That number of men was too many for one commanding officer to handle, so I decided to divide my army into three corps. Then each corps or wing would have 20,000 men, a more reasonable amount to handle.

Longstreet already led 1st Corps, so I left him in charge of that one. Even though, General Ewell had lost a leg at Second Manassas, I knew he had served admirably under Jackson, and also he knew the tactics and the men of 2nd Corps. So it was a natural for me to have him move up to command the 2nd Corps. For leader of the newly developed corps, I chose an aggressive and ferocious fighter, A. P. Hill to lead 3rd Corps. I knew he was occasionally ill, and that he was an impatient man. I also knew that he had even attacked the Yankees several times without orders; but his ferocity in battle superseded those faults and led me to put him in a command position.

I also added four more cavalry brigades under the command of General Jeb Stuart. One of the brigades I sent was led by General Grumble Jones whom I knew did not get along with Stuart.[32] Rumor had it the feeling was mutual, but I thought by this time in the war, both men had mellowed. I was wrong.

During a skirmish at St. James Church,[33] Grumble Jones sent word by courier to Stuart telling him a column of Yanks were coming at him on his flank. Stuart sent this incredulous reply back:

Tell General Jones to watch the Yankees at his front. I'll watch the flanks.

---

[32] General William "Grumble" Jones was serving in California and had just married a most beautiful woman when he was ordered to return to Washington. The ship the couple was on ran into a monstrous storm. To avoid the water rushing into their cabin Jones and his bride scrambled up on deck. While Jones was holding on to her in the windstorm, a horrific wave ripped her from his arms and dashed her overboard. An agonized Jones then turned bitter and was never the same again.

[33] Not only was Jeb Stuart surprised and humiliated by the Federal Cavalry at Brandy Station, but General Lee's 26-year-old son Rooney was wounded in the thigh as he led his brigade in a final charge.

When he got the note back Jones remarked to the courier, "So he thinks they ain't comin', does he? Well, let him alone, he'll damned soon see for himself."

I should have known better and kept them apart. Even the way they dressed was an obvious clue to their differences. Stuart, may God rest his soul, was gregarious, with his cavalry hat, the brim turned up on the right side pinned there with a yellow star and the plumed hawks feather trailing behind. When I close my eyes I can still see him in his long frockcoat and gold striped pants, tapping his foot to Sweeney's fast rhythms on his mandolin. On the other hand, there was Grumble Jones always wearing the same outfit: an old worn out slouch hat, blue jeans and a homespun shirt. I should have known better...

****

In Washington, something seemingly inconsequential was taking place that would later prove to have grave consequences for us. It appears that General Couch was so outraged at Hookers vacillations during the

Battle of Chancellorsville that he refused to stay under Hooker's command. He was immediately transferred and replaced by General Winfield Scott Hancock. In retrospect it turns out that, in my opinion, it may very well be that General Hancock was the one man among many, who with his military brilliance tipped the scale against us at Gettysburg.

But I had such high hopes that Gettysburg would be the last battle. In a private meeting with General Isaac Trimble the week before the battle, I expressed to him how I hoped to sequentially wreck the seven corps of the Federal Army:

"Our army is in good spirits, Trimble, and can be concentrated in twenty-four hours. When the Federals find out where we are in Pennsylvania, they will make forced marches to interpose between us and Baltimore, and Philadelphia, and even Washington. They will come up strung out in a long line, weary and very much demoralized by the time they get to Pennsylvania. Then I will attack them. I will throw an overwhelming force on their advance, crush it and drive one corps back on another, and by successive blows create a panic and virtually destroy their army.

Then, Trimble, when the Northern people get the casualty lists and count the dead and wounded, we shall be able to secede from the Union."

****

While Stuart was protecting my army from Federal Cavalry hit and run tactics he smoldered from resentment caused by criticism, not only from his fellow officers, but also from prominent newspapers like the *Richmond Examiner* and the *Sentinel.*

Holding off Pleasonton's Federal Cavalry in a series of vicious cavalry skirmishes in Loudoun Valley,[34] Stuart was well satisfied that he had protected my army from Yankee eyes. He was so satisfied that he approached me with an idea that he thought would not only help the Confederate cause, but bring back his celebrated reputation.

---

[34] The battles in Loudoun Valley bolstered the Northern Cavalry troop's confidence at the defeat of Stuart's Cavalry who, before the Battle of Brandy Station, were considered invincible.

As the sun set in the twilight, Stuart came to me at my headquarters tent and urged me to let him harass Joe Hooker and delay the Federal Army's pursuit.

Although my first inclination was to keep the cavalry with me into Pennsylvania, I thought his suggestion over for a while and realized his proposal had some merit. But knowing his fondness for spectacle, I stipulated, and put it in writing, that as soon as Hooker crossed the Potomac, Stuart was to immediately come back and take his position on my right flank. I told him emphatically, "If Hooker doesn't move, then and only then, you may go around him and do as much damage as possible. But if he does move across that river you must also move back. In either case, as soon as YOU re-cross the Potomac, you must join Ewell on my flank immediately.

It was a conversation with a subordinate I will regret for the rest of my life.[35]

Slowly and carefully I got my army ready to leave the Rappahannock and head north.

---

[35] For eight days from the time of the written order, General Stuart, the eyes and ears of Lee's army upon whom he relied for information about the enemy's movements, might as well have been on another continent.

Just as I was getting Traveller saddled, Major Taylor tapped me on the shoulder.

"General Lee," he said pointing upward to the sky, "look at that!"

I leaned back and looked upward. There it was a great balloon, just over our heads, watching our every move. I had heard a private person named Thaddeus Lowe had made these balloons and outfitted the Federals with several of them. I turned back to Taylor and shook my head. Major this is a new innovation we must counter. Thaddeus Lowe doesn't own the sky. We must get our own squadron of balloonists to counter the Yanks. Why don't you report this to President Davis and see if we can get started creating our own unit of balloons for observation of those people. Tell him about Bryant and his Confederate balloon and how he helped us before."

Meanwhile my men got on the road and were soon enjoying the march. After a while the balloons were gone and we continued north.

When we reached the Maryland border and crossed the Potomac I saw an amusing sight. When General George (Maryland)

Steuart reached the far bank, he joyfully leaped from his horse, kissed the ground and stood on his head. He surely loved his home state.

The army was now moving so fast, one soldier's journal I later saw said: "we had breakfast in Virginia, whiskey in Maryland, and supper in Pennsylvania."

It wasn't long before the entire Confederate Army was in Pennsylvania with General Jenkins in the lead just four miles from Harrisburg, the capitol of Pennsylvania and the high mark of the Confederacy on Northern soil.

****

The scout Harrison was a stooped, scruffy man, a shadowy character, who had been arrested by my pickets when he tried to steal by them near my headquarters tent. Instead of shooting him on the spot, a thoughtful sergeant listened to the ragged man's story and brought him to Colonel Sorrel, General Longstreet's chief of staff.

After laughing heartily with the dirty, ragged scout, the colonel ordered the sergeant to get the prisoner some food, and before he met with Longstreet and me, a clean uniform. When the sergeant said there wasn't a clean uniform in the entire army, they fed him and then brought the scout directly to me.

Now I was being told by this ragged scarecrow that Hooker's army was moving north to get in front of me and had contacted another two Federal corps, already encamped near Frederick, Maryland, to get in my rear. I have no confidence in any scout other than my own cavalry trained and proven by me, much less than this bedraggled, unmilitary figure in front of me. So many spies, through the centuries, have given information to both sides for the money involved. Not impressed by his story, I said as much to him.

Harrison ignored my detrimental statement and spoke up. "Not only are the Yanks concentrating their troops, but I saw other Federal troops heading toward South Mountain. And by the way there's more news. They have sacked Hooker and put in his place a new commander by the name of Meade."

This latest bit of news brought me up short. "Meade, you say!" Then to myself I muttered: "I know him, and I will tell all who will listen, Meade will make no error at my front. I will sorely miss Hooker." I turned to my aide, Colonel Taylor, "Give this man some food and get him something to wear."

I've already eaten, Gen'ral but I sure could use somethin' ter drink.

Taylor smiled and with a wave of his hand dismissed the sergeant and Harrison. "I'll take care of him General Lee," he said to me and also left.

After they were gone I turned to another aide. "Colonel Venable, go and see General Longstreet and see if he will vouch for this scout. Come back at once and tell me what he says."

In a few minutes, Venable returned. He saluted and said, "General Longstreet says Harrison is completely reliable. If he tells you something, treat it like the gospel."[36]

---

[36] Not only was Harrison reliable, he was able to move freely among the Federals because of his acting ability. Although history has never documented his contributions to the Southern cause, after the war a former Confederate officer saw him in a play in Baltimore. When the play ended the officer went back stage. After being cordial Harrison said he was in want and borrowed $10. History then swallowed him up and he was never heard of again.

On the other hand, for the Union, another civilian, John Burns, a 70-year-old veteran of the war of 1812, jumped in to the Federal line at

Since General Stuart has been gone for days, and thus I have no reliable eyes and ears following the Federal Army, I must accept the word of this scout's report.

I then told Colonel Venable to make up an order in my name to have all three of our corps concentrate in such a manner as to prevent the Federals from interfering with our communications with Virginia.

As I was told, Meade was now in charge and got his army going the very next morning. Meanwhile Longstreet and Hill had made camp just east of Chambersburg. But the Federal Cavalry headed by John Buford stole a march on all of us and entered Gettysburg near noon on June 30th. Little did I know that General Pettigrew of Heth's Division was also going into Gettysburg to find some shoes.

When Pettigrew saw Buford's cavalry, and because I gave orders for our men not to look for a fight, he beat a quick retreat. When he got back to General Heth's headquarters he reported what he had seen. While he was

---

McPherson's Ridge, on July 1st and fought valiantly against the Rebels all the way to Pickett's Charge on July 3rd. He was wounded three times during the three days and earned the praise of Lincoln himself, in person.

telling Heth about Buford, General Hill came up and listened to the conversation.

When Pettigrew finished, Hill said to Heth, "That's nonsense, the enemy is still at Middleburg and have not even struck their tents yet."

Heth then said, "Well then, if there are no Yankees in Gettysburg, and you have no objection, Sir, I will go and get those shoes tomorrow."[37]

"I assure you there are no Yankees there. I have not one objection in the world."

****

Watching Pettigrew retreating earlier, one of Buford's Brigadiers said to General Buford, "They won't return."

Buford smiled and said, "General, get your men dug in. Not only will they return but they will come in the morning and they will come booming skirmishers three deep. And

---

[37] Heth probably made the shoe story up. Since there were no shoe factories in Gettysburg it's more likely that General Heth was looking less for shoes and more for trouble.

you will have to fight like the Devil until support arrives."

****

As I understand it, a Lieutenant Marcellus Jones of the 8th Illinois Cavalry, saw our boys through the mist at 5:30 in the morning, coming from Cashtown. The Lieutenant was just three miles from Gettysburg and thought it best to call his pickets in and go tell headquarters what he was seeing. Just then an officer leading the Confederate column came out of the mist. Without another thought Lieutenant Jones borrowed his sergeant's carbine, aimed at the Rebel officer and fired. The mist then closed up around the officer, but the shot fired stirred up a Confederate hornet's nest. As Jones and his men withdrew, the Rebels started firing back. This was the beginning of a monumental battle that would decide the outcome of the war.

This is when I needed Stuart and, bless his honored soul, he failed me. It was the first day of July and here I was, unfamiliar with the territory and knew even less about my enemy's strength. I had no other choice but to order my army to enter into no general engagement until my three corps were concentrated near Gettysburg.

It was a tedious wait for me as General Longstreet was a day's march away and General Ewell was several hours north.

Meanwhile General Meade had his engineers laying out a defensive line along Pipe Creek 20 miles from Gettysburg, and he had told his generals it was to be a fallback position in case they needed it.

But the battle was already out of Meade's hands as well as mine. General Heth had run into Buford's dismounted Cavalry, instead of shoes, on Herr Ridge. This battle began just one and a half miles from Gettysburg.

The first of Heth's brigades was led by Joseph Davis, a nephew of the president. He was followed up by General Archer, who ignored his friend Pettigrew when he told him there was trouble ahead. Archer was later captured. Pettigrew was right. Buford and his men were ready for Heth. I was told Buford said, "My arrangements were made for entertaining him." (Heth)

Firing furiously using their breech loading carbines, (together with a battery of horse artillery), Buford's[38] men held up Heth's advance for more than an hour.

General Reynolds finally arrived with reinforcements and conferred with Buford. Then Reynolds dashed on horseback to his two corps, got them off the road and led them across the fields toward the ridge and the now raging battle. By 10 a.m. Reynolds men got to the crest and charged into battle. Unfortunately as General Reynolds was placing the men of the Iron Brigade on the ridge, a Minié ball caught him behind the right ear. He was dead before he hit the ground.

While his staff was gathering around Reynold's body, the Iron Brigade was turning Archer's flank, scattering the Rebels and capturing Archer.

Archer later told me, "When I was brought to Doubleday's headquarters,

---

[38] After graduating West Point, John Buford saw lots of action on the frontier. He served with distinction at 2nd Bull Run and was badly wounded there. His valor and generalship at Gettysburg gave him even more distinction. Unfortunately for the Union, he contracted Typhoid Fever in the autumn of 1863 and died soon after.

Doubleday said, 'Good morning Archer, I'm glad to see you.' I quickly replied, "Well, I'm *not* glad to see you by a damned sight."

Accompanied by Longstreet and the men of First Corps, I rode towards Gettysburg. Soon I was anxiously riding toward the sound of the guns. When I reached Herr Ridge, I found a dazed Heth trying to reform his shaken division.[39]

One of his men falling back and firing at Buford's men saw me and said, "Better fall back, Gen'ral Lee. Them Yankee boys shootin' at us ain't no militia, them's those damned black-hatted fellers."

I quietly told him to join his company and that I would soon join him. When General Heth saw me, he requested permission to attack again. I said, "No, I am not prepared to bring on a general engagement today. Longstreet is not yet completely up... But just then Jubal Early, leading his division, showed up on the battlefield. Now the engagement changed from retreat to opportunity. Without

[39] Heth's division had suffered a serious number of casualties caused by the furious fighting of a roused Army of the Potomac fighting on their home soil.

being told, Early's men jumped into the fray on the Federal right. I thought, *If General Hill*[40] *could renew his assault on the left.*

As soon as Hill straightened his line and attacked the Federal left, I saw a pincer movement developing. Now if Hill and Early would press those people, the Federals would be caught in the steel jaws of a Confederate alligator. Early and John B. Gordon attacked together with accompanying cannon and infantry, guns and rifles blazing. For a few minutes the Federals held, but then, Gordon, standing in his stirrups of his coal black stallion, and waving Early's men on with his black slouch hat, inspired his men to drive the Yankees off the hill and made them skedaddle toward Gettysburg.

It was just at that moment that Gordon saw a Federal officer lying on the ground, his chest red with blood. Thinking the man had only a short time to live Gordon dismounted

[40] A.P. Hill suffered from several ailments (Some may have been psychosomatic) He was given Third Corps, which he led into Gettysburg. His newness at corps command may have been the reason for his mediocre performance at Gettysburg, although he displayed excellent skill in later battles. He was mortally wounded at the battle of Petersburg.

and went to him. He gave the wounded man some water and asked his name. "Francis C. Barlow," was the answer. The officer then weakly grasped Gordon's arm. "Would you be kind enough to send word to Mrs. Barlow and tell her my dying thoughts were of her?" He coughed up some frothy blood and clutched his chest. "She is at Meade's headquarters tent."

"I will," Gordon said. And he did.[41]

By now the entire line of Federals was broken and streaming toward Gettysburg.

One of my officers standing nearby then said emphatically, "It looks indeed as if the end of the war has come!"

But it wasn't over yet. Heth's men moved off Herr Ridge to chase the fleeing Yankees but were stopped cold by the Iron Brigade. It was a costly stop as they had 1,153 casualties out of 1,829 men. But Heth and 1,500 of his men were also casualties. In the 26th North Carolina regiment only 212 men survived

---

[41] Gordon carried Barlow to a shade tree and gave him water from his canteen. Barlow asked if Gordon would contact his wife. Gordon said he would and would tell her how bravely he died. But Barlow survived and one can only imagine the shock of both men when they met on a Washington street after the war. They remained good friends thereafter.

their assault, a casualty rate of 75 percent. The battle of Herr Ridge was a bloodbath.

After that the Federals started to retreat slowly and in good order firing as they went. When my boys saw that, they started to push harder. Soon the trickle of retreat became a rout as the Federal troops began to run toward Gettysburg. We poured shot and shell into the chaos of the retreat until there were bodies and wreckage everywhere. Our men cheered until they were hoarse. I was pleased with the result, but sad at all the carnage.

It was then that Winfield Scott Hancock showed up on the field. The beginning of his command was awkward for Hancock, as General Oliver Howard, who was then in charge, outranked Hancock. But somehow in the midst of all that chaos, they worked it out and Hancock took over. He looked over the terrain and saw Cemetery Ridge, Cemetery Ridge and the Round Tops, pointed to them and said, "There is a strong position. Let's get everyone up there and dig in."

After he formed his defensive line and sent for reinforcement troops, Hancock then sat down on a stone fence and studied my Confederate troops facing him.

I saw the advantage of having the high ground the Federals now had and urged A. P. Hill to immediately renew the attack. To my amazement he declined, stating that, "My troops are bloodied, exhausted and almost out of ammunition. Since he was my most combative Commander, I had no doubt Hill was sincere. This left me no alternative but to call upon General Ewell to assault the Federals, chase the frightened and demoralized Yankees off the high ground, take Gettysburg and then Washington to finally end this bloody war.

Meanwhile I was not the only one that saw the opportunity. Both Gordon and Early urged Ewell to take the heights. He answered them by saying, "General Lee told me to come to Gettysburg, but gave me no orders to go further." General Trimble then came up and asked forcefully for Ewell to allow him to take Culp's Hill. When Ewell refused, Trimble stormed away in a fury, uttering unspeakable oaths.

Without taking time to dictate and write a written order, I gave Major Walter Taylor a verbal one. *Tell General Ewell the Federals are in headlong flight. It is only necessary to press those people in order to secure possession of those heights. It is the commanding general's wish that you should do so,* IF PRACTICABLE.

I have wished to God a million times since that day I had not uttered those two last words.

I waited for over an hour for Ewell to start the attack. By 7 p.m. my patience at an end and I started for Ewell's headquarters. By the time I got there, I looked up at the heights, saw the Yankees digging away, with more troops arriving on Cemetery Hill. I shook my head in despair and went back to my tent. The opportunity was gone.

That night, at midnight, Meade called a meeting of his Federal officers. All of them agreed the heights were the best place to fight the next battle.[42]

---

[42] Two of Meade's sisters were married to Rebel soldiers and were ardent secessionists. Also his wife's sister was married to Governor Henry Wise of Virginia who had signed the death warrant for John Brown. Wise was later a Confederate brigadier general.

Where is Longstreet?[43]

Robert E. Lee

Chapter 20: Gettysburg

The Second Day, July 2nd, 1863

At 3:30 a.m. on July 2nd, I was on my feet after only three hours of sleep. There was much to do. I woke major Veneble and asked him to send me two officers for a mission. In half an hour two lieutenants stood before me sleepy-eyed. After I returned their salutes I said, “Good morning gentlemen, I am very sorry to wake you so early but it seems the war won’t wait.

One lieutenant named Murphy shook his freckled faced head and said, “Jayzes Christ,

[43] On the second day General James Longstreet, failed to properly execute Lee’s orders and marched his men away from the battle site, while Federal forces collected to fend off a major Confederate assault.

Gen'ral, 'tis a wee bit early ter be gaddin' about, don't yer think?

The other man chimed in. "Yes, General Lee, me an' Murph here had a hard day yesterday an' the major wasn't gentle-like when he woke us. Dumped me outta me bed he did."

I laughed heartily. "Fortunes of war lads, fortunes of war." Then I got serious. "The Yankees are digging away on Cemetery Ridge and Cemetery Hill. If we're going to make them run we have to take those heights. That's why I waked you both. I want you to make a complete reconnaissance of Cemetery Ridge, Cemetery Hill and the two Round Tops and then report back to me."

"Well, General, if it's important then you got the two best men in the army to do the deed. Me an' Murph will be back shortly with the information." The two men saluted and before I could answer they were gone.

I then mounted Traveller and rode over to Seminary Ridge. With my binoculars I surveyed the Federal Troop dispositions on Cemetery Hill. It was then that I discovered that the Federal line did not extend to the Round Tops.

Plans for a decisive attack began to form in my head as I returned to the headquarters tent. Soon after I got there my generals started to join me. Longstreet entered first and began by again suggesting a move to the left. I politely but definitely rejected his suggestion once more. By that time all the other generals joined us. Some sat down on a fallen log and some on field chairs. They soon started suggesting their ideas and strategies.

I thanked them but depending what my two scouts will tell me, my plan was almost complete. I then laid my battle plan before the generals.

"At daybreak tomorrow, I will order General Longstreet, to march south to Cemetery Ridge and then, from there, he and General A. P. Hill will simultaneously attack Cemetery Hill." I further told them the attack must be made in echelon, each brigade in turn striking the Federal line. "Before the assault starts General Ewell will feint with a demonstration of force. Then if the opportunity presents, Ewell will charge up and take Culp's Hill. Of course the final plan must wait until my scouts report."

I must have looked ill by the time I finished explaining my plan as the generals were looking at me oddly. Longstreet asked if I felt all right and I brushed off the suggestion saying I felt fine. But that was not the case. The pain in my chest and arm had returned and I felt weak and disoriented. I had slept only three hours that night and after tossing and turning in my cot for the last half hour. I still felt ill.

I dismissed the generals and called the corporal standing guard outside my tent and bade him to get Major Taylor. When Taylor arrived I told him to get my horse. "I want to go to back to Seminary Ridge, and with my binoculars, view the latest Federal dispositions on Cemetery Hill."

After watching the Federals dig in on Cemetery Hill I returned to my tent and paced the dirt floor stopping every few moments to glare at the entrance flaps. Then I began pacing again thinking only, *where is that damn Stuart?*[44]

---

[44] Major General Henry Heth said: General Lee discussed the absence of Stuart with every officer who visited him. He would say, "Where on earth is my cavalry?" or "Can you tell me where General Stuart is?" To say he

****

The next day started badly. Not only were all my troops not up, but as soon as he saw me, Longstreet again began to press me to go around the Federal left.

I courteously refused saying, "Without Stuart, we would be in strange territory and would be risking entrapment."

By now only Pickett and McLaws had yet to join us and I paced anxiously waiting their arrival. I then heard Longstreet whisper to Hood, "The general is a bit nervous this morning. He wishes me to attack. But I do not wish to do much fighting without Pickett. I never like to go into battle with one boot off."

When McLaws arrived, I ordered him to array his troops across Emmitsburg Road. Unbelievably, Longstreet jumped in and countermanded my order. And in front of the other men. I then angrily restated the order. To save further argument, McLaws saluted and said, "Yessir" to me. Without looking at Longstreet McLaws left us.

---

was distraught over the situation is an understatement.

I suppose I looked calm, but on the inside I was shaking with anger. This insubordination on the part of Longstreet was an ominous beginning of things to come.

Just then the two officers I sent to reconnoiter the Round Tops showed up. They reported to me, confirming what I had seen.

"Jayzes, Joseph an' Mary, Gen'ral, I'm sure glad you sent us up there. It looks busy but they's only pickets blockin' the way..." Then the other officer chimed in, "And more important, sir, both Little and Big Round Tops are unoccupied."

That news completed my plan of attack. I reiterated my orders of yesterday to my generals. Longstreet and Hill were to attack Cemetery Ridge and Cemetery Hill in echelon striking the Federal line in a series of trip-hammer blows. Just before that attack Ewell would make a demonstration at the sound of the guns. And if opportunity presented itself he would attack Culp's Hill. And that should vacate the hills and make the Yanks skedaddle. Once we had the heights Gettysburg would be ours. Longstreet and Hill then discussed the battle plan with me for a few minutes making sure they understood exactly what I wanted. I could see by the impression on his face that Longstreet was still smarting at my refusal to change the plan but it was too late to do anything about it. Precisely at 10 a.m. July 2nd, I turned to the morose Longstreet and said, "I think you better move on." I then rode over to Ewell's ambulance to discuss his role in my plan. When I got back, to my disappointment, Longstreet had not even started his march toward his attack jump off point. He said he was waiting for Law's brigade. Law did not arrive for another hour.

****

It was noon before Longstreet's 1st Corps started to finally get underway.[45] Even then he was delayed and was not ready until late in the afternoon.

---

[45] Several of his fellow officers were critical of a headstrong James Longstreet during the Battle of Gettysburg. Even students of the Civil War say that his lateness, hesitation to attack, and downright disobedience on August 29th, 1862 at the second battle of Manassas were an omen of his quarrelsome acts that came later during the Battle of Gettysburg. The kernels of much of the disaster at Gettysburg were planted in that moment when Lee gave in to Longstreet at Manassas, and Longstreet realized that he would.

I started back to my tent to be available for reports of the battle. All the way back, and even when I entered my tent I thought of only one thing. *Where the devil is JEB Stuart*? My mind wandered. *The enemy must still be in Virginia, that's why I have not heard from Stuart.*[46]

Then, as if in answer to my angry thoughts, I heard a horse gallop up. Voices outside the tent exchanged greetings and Stuart himself parted the tent flaps and stepped inside. He was smiling but when he saw my face his smile quickly faded.

I was well aware my countenance bore a look of frigid disapproval, but that's exactly the way I felt.

Colonel Taylor stood at his field desk watching my face turn several shades of red, and tried to figure a way to allay the storm he knew was coming.

When the tent flaps had parted, Taylor stood up. Then when Stuart's smiling face showed at the opening. Taylor saw my neck,

---

[46] A Gettysburg physician who called on Lee at this time, thought him agitated and deeply disturbed.

turn bright scarlet and began to spasm. Taylor then knew it was too late to save Stuart from my impending wrath and he quickly sat down.

Stuart took a step forward and saluted. I took a step toward him and raised my right hand balled into a fist. Taylor was sure that I was going to strike a surprised Stuart.

My fist started forward in an arc calculated to strike the unflinching Stuart's face. But halfway to General Stuart, my arm stopped, trembled a bit and then, after a few seconds, fell to my side. I gave a withering look at Stuart and then turned and began to pace again.

When Lee's back was to him Stuart turned to Taylor and shrugged his shoulders, a puzzled, questioning look on his face. Taylor grimaced, shook his head and looked down at his papers, all moves calculated to let General Stuart know he was on his own.

I turned to Stuart and glared at him. "General Stuart, where in Hell have you been?[47]

---

[47] Lee was terribly angry because he had been forced to fight before he was ready and more importantly because he had not felt free to maneuver because of lack of Stuart's scouting.

Do you know that you are the eyes and ears of my army and I have not heard a word from you for 10 days?"[48]

"B-B-But, General Lee," a stuttering Stuart said, "I have brought you 125 wagons loaded with supplies and their teams..."

"Yes, General Stuart," I said viciously, "but they are an impediment to me now. Dammit, I have invaded the enemy country with a blindfold on. I have no idea where Hooker is and what he is doing."

Suddenly I saw the light go out in the eyes of this fine officer and my heart constricted in my chest. My voice softened as I took his hand. "Let me ask your help now," I said softly.

Taylor looked at me in disbelief.

Stuart looked away with the face of a punished boy about to get a reprieve.

"We will not discuss this further," I said. "Just help me fight those people now."

---

[48] Lee did have a small cavalry unit still with him after Stuart left, but as Sorrel pointed out after the battle, "It was the great body of that splendid horse under their leader, Stuart, that Lee wanted. He was the eyes and ears of Lee's army and the strong right arm of the commander...

Taylor shook his head and buried himself in his paperwork. He told me later he thought to himself, *I wish General Lee could use Stuart's troops right away, but his men are so strung out and exhausted it will take them hours just to get back to camp. We will have to wait until tomorrow to use Stuart's troops again.*

Stuart saluted and sheepishly left the tent.

After he was gone, I waited somewhat impatiently for word from Longstreet. Little did I know he had run into several frustrating events in getting his two divisions ready for their assault. To my dismay I was informed that Longstreet's men finally got ready to fight at 3:30 p.m.[49] I shook my head and thought to myself, *Would these subordinates ever be on time?*

Longstreet arrayed his corps with Hood on the right and McLaws on the left.

McLaws had been told there would be little opposition at his front but when he walked to the edge of the wood where his

---

[49] Lonstreet was supposed to be ready at 10:30 a.m. He was 5 hours late.

troops were concealed he found an astonishing sight. The unsettling sight McLaws saw were the troops of General Dan Sickles[50] massed in his front. The placing of his troops in that place was a mistake by General Sickles. But it was a fortunate error as it threw off McLaws battle timetable and knocked my plan completely askew. Instead of McLaws having a vulnerable Federal flank on Cemetery Ridge, McLaws would have 10,000 battle-hardened Union troopers to fight through.

McLaws sent three messages to Longstreet about the veteran army at his front, but was told by Longstreet he must attack when the time came.

I made two mistakes for this assault. First, I gave verbal orders not written ones. Secondly, during the attack I acted as my own courier, riding back and forth between Longstreet, Hill and Ewell. That took more time than I thought it would.

---

[50] Dan Sickles on Feb. 27, 1859 had murdered his friend, Phillip Key, son of Francis Scott Key, the composer of the *Star Spangled Banner*. He shot Key when he found out that Phillip Key was his wife's lover. At his trial his lawyer's defense was *temporary insanity*. (It was the first time that had ever been used). He got off on that defense with public support, but the public was incensed when he later reconciled with his unfaithful wife.

On top of all of that, during this battle I had severe chest pains and even more severe diarrhea.

****

That morning General Meade found out that Sickles had moved ahead of the army and rode over to him. When Meade reached Sickles, he said angrily, “General, you are too far out. In fact Sickles, you have moved a half-mile in front of the rest of the Federal Army.

Sickles, finally realizing his mistake said, Yes General Meade. Shall I move back?”

“I wish to God you could, he shouted, but those people will not permit it.”

Just then a Confederate bomb burst near Meade’s horse, Baldy. Maddened by the bomb Baldy took off for the rear. It was a while until Meade could get control of the horse again.

Looking down at Sickles from Cemetery Hill, General Hancock shook his head at Sickles folly. “Wait a moment,” he said to his aide, “when Johnny Reb gets a twist on him, you’ll soon see him come tumbling back.”

General Hood was having similar problems on the Confederate right. Facing increasing numbers of Federal troops, Hood decided to ignore specific orders and go around to attack the enemy on his flank and rear. Twice he notified Longstreet of his desire to change his orders, and twice he was refused. Finally, looking at the bristling Yankee guns at his front, and the carnage they could cause, Hood decided to ignore his orders and launched his attack around to the left toward Devil's Den and the flank of the Federal line.

While Hood was advancing around the Federal left, Colonel William Oates and his men of the 15th Alabama, contrary to reports found Federal troops there when they started fighting their way up Big Round Top. After taking a toll of Oates' men, the Federals, unable to withstand the Confederate charges, retreated off Big Round Top and Oates and his men took the hill. When they got to the top most of the men were on their knees sobbing for breath.

When he recovered, Oates went to the edge and looked down. He could see the Federals digging in on Little Round Top 100 feet below. *If I could get a couple of 10 pounders up here I could enfilade the whole*

Yankee line and get them off the heights in a hurry.

Just then Captain Terrell showed up on horseback with terrible news. “General Hood had lost his arm to a shell and General Law is now in command.” His order was for Oates and his men to forget Big Round Top and capture Little Round Top.

Always a man to obey orders, Oates reluctantly left Big Round Top and started toward the lower hill.

When the men of the 15th Alabama tried to take Little Round Top, they were met by a ferocious line of Federal soldiers determined not to give way. The Federals had gotten there just a few minutes before the 15th Alabama arrived. It seems that General Gouverneur Warren saw that Little Round Top was occupied by just a few Union signalmen. He also saw that Little Round Top was the key to keeping the heights from the Confederates. Warren sent a courier to Meade requesting a division be sent to Little Round Top. Meade finally got word to Colonel Strong Vincent. Reacting quickly, Colonel Vincent immediately got his men up to Little Round Top and deployed them behind some boulders.

Among Colonel Vincent's four regiments was the 20th Maine led by former Professor and now Colonel Joshua Chamberlain.[51] Vincent placed them on the left of his line and told Chamberlain, "This is the left of the Federal Army and you are the end of the line. You must hold this ground at all costs."

Before Chamberlain could answer Vincent or even take another breath, the air was full of iron. The 15th Alabama was attacking.

For the next hour and a half the fighting that took place was best described by Private Gerrish of the 20th Maine.

The air seemed alive with lead. Men shouted, groaned and cursed and died.

---

[51] Chamberlain was a professor of rhetoric and languages at Bowdoin College in Maine. In 1862, he was granted a sabbatical to study abroad but instead joined the Union Army. He fought in 24 engagements but is chiefly remembered for his gallant defense of Little Round Top at Gettysburg on the 2nd day. At the Appomattox surrender, Chamberlain was given the honor of accepting the surrender of the, Army of Northern Virginia. Post war he was elected governor of Maine. He then returned to Bowdoin College and soon became its president.

The Confederates made charge after charge trying to dislodge the boys from Maine. They would not be moved.

Colonel Oates' brother John was shot and fell and died right in front of him. Oates, with tears in his eyes touched the body and then led the last charge up the hill shouting, "Forward my men!"

Out of ammunition, Chamberlain now gave his last order. "Men, fix bayonets. They are as tired as we are, but we will have a downhill run." Chamberlain stood tall and pulled his sword out of its scabbard and yelled, "All right men, CHARGE!" But no one moved.

Suddenly Lieutenant Melcher took a step forward and hollered, "Come on boys!" After a few seconds he was joined by, Chamberlain waving his drawn sword. Then with a roar, the entire surviving men of the 20th Maine charged downhill into the troops from Alabama.

While the 20th Maine came charging down at the 15th Alabama, other Federal troops moved on their rear and flank. Bullets came whizzing at Oates' men from all three sides accompanied by the crazy men coming at them from the top of the hill. It was too much.[52] The Confederates still standing turned and began running back down the hill. Those unable to outrun the Maine boys surrendered en masse. Many of those who thought they were saved by running laterally were shot down by the other Federal troops.

Although the Alabama boys had a rough handling by the 20th Maine, all along the rest of the front it seemed it was our day. But as I watched through my binoculars I saw a distressing sight, both Hancock and Warren were like racehorses propping up one force about to run, then going quickly to another to find support for them. I actually watched General Warren helping a lieutenant manhandle a gun to the top of Little Round Top and then scurry down looking for reinforcements.

He soon found Paddy O'Rorke. Warren recently told me in a letter that he said to O'Rorke, "Paddy, I need you on the top of Little Round Top in a hurry." O'Rorke saluted, gave the order and he and his men raced to

---

[52] One captured Confederate soldier said, "Many must be the desolate homes and orphan children of the South that will rue that rash charge at Little Round Top."

the top of the Hill and smashed into Robertson's Texans driving them back down the slope. I am terribly sorry to report that the valiant Colonel O'Rorke was killed in that charge.

Just to the left of Little Round Top was a stretch of Hell called the Devil's Den. Here is where Confederate General Beverly Robertson[53] found himself after being pushed off Little Round Top and here is where he fought the "Orange Blossoms".[54]

Devils Den was a kaleidoscope of rocks and boulders, caves and paths where a man could hide or get behind a boulder and become a sniper. General Robertson told me, "The Federals had six guns placed strategically just waiting for us."

General Robertson led his Texans, Georgians and Arkansas men in a spine

---

[53] General Robertson led a multiple life moving to Texas after becoming a medical doctor, then an Indian fighter and finally a politician. He was wounded at Devil's Den in 1863.

[54] The regiment of the 124th New York was made up of men from Orange County. They wore orange ribbons on their coats and called themselves the "Orange Blossoms".

chilling, Rebel Yell charge right into the Federal Guns.

It was well that General Robertson had been an Indian fighter as the battle in Devil's Den became just that, a wild melee reminiscent of an Indian free-for-all.

The struggle was hand-to-hand, muzzle-to-muzzle and bayonet-to-bayonet. And the small stream running through Devil's Den was soon red with blood.

That morning before the battle started I had a strange feeling of foreboding and made an observation to General Ewell, "General Meade has the advantage of us in a shorter and inside line, and we are too extended."[55]

What happened during the battle on July 2nd was just what I feared. Meade did indeed make use of his shorter line borrowing from quiet areas and sending those men to hot spots along the line. General Meade had another weapon on Cemetery Ridge, and that

---

55 In fact Meade's hook-shaped line of Federals was 3 miles long and had the inside curve, while the Confederate army formed a line that was 5 miles long on the outside. For Meade, moving a unit of men from one end (Culp's Hill) to another (where the 20th Maine was stationed) would take only 20 minutes.

was General Winfield Scott Hancock.[56] When we finally got all of our men to follow the plan of the echelon attack, it was Hancock that used his skill and courage, shifting his Federal army to parry our spirited assaults. A good example of Hancock's military skill and bravery was when General Barksdale and his Mississippians made a ferocious charge up Cemetery Ridge. Their only opposition to their charge was Bigelow's artillery of six 12 pounders on the Plumb Run line.

Barksdale's men raced up Cemetery Ridge, and ran into Colonel Bigelow's guns loaded with canister. For a while the guns held off Barksdale's men, but slowly and surely the Confederates started to gain the advantage. As the Confederates overlapped

---

[56] On June 15th, 1861 General Winfield Scott Hancock, and his wife Almira, presided over the famous goodbye dinner for Lo Armistead and several other Southerners leaving to join the Confederate army. At Gettysburg on July 1st, Hancock was responsible for stopping the Union retreat from turning into a rout. On July 2nd, he managed brilliantly when the Federal third corps collapsed. But it was on July 3rd when his bravery and courage helped break Pickett's charge and turn near defeat into a Federal victory. Armistead, though dying, asked for him, but a bomb had landed near Hancock's saddle and had driven the nails of the saddle into his groin. He lived, but never saw Armistead. The battle for Gettysburg was over for him.

him, to save his guns Bigelow prepared to pack up his guns and retreat. Just then Lieutenant Colonel McGilvery came up the hill, saw Bigelow and urged him to stay put. "If we don't stop them," McGilvery shouted above the noise of the guns, "there would be no one to stop the Rebels from breaking the main Union line on Cemetery Ridge."

Bigelow started to answer, "But Colonel, we have no infantry to protect the guns…"

"My guns are coming up. We'll back you up and send the Rebels to Hell."

But soon the Federals were down to two guns and the end seemed near. That's when General Hancock came up with Federal reinforcements. In a few moments General Hancock himself led the charge down the slope of Cemetery Ridge, crashed through the thicket lining Plumb Run, and smashed into the center of Barksdale's brigade. Barksdale was killed[57] and his shocked brigade retreated in a near rout.

---

[57] The legend goes that the Federal Generals were so afraid of Barksdale they ordered every Federal Soldier in one company to shoot at the Rebel Commander. They were successful and the aggressive Rebel Commander died later that night just after saying to the Federal surgeon treating him,

Finally my army began to utilize my echelon plan and with several trip-hammer blows forced the Federal third corps to speedily retreat.

It was then that I saw we could gain Cemetery Ridge. I immediately wrote an order and gave it to a courier to bring to Barksdale's Mississippians. I wrote:

Take that ridge before those people bring up reinforcements.

But Barksdale was dead and Hancock saw what I was doing. To gain a few minutes until he could get reinforcements to take the place of the retreating Federals, he mounted his horse and galloped over to the 1st Minnesota and confronted a Colonel Colvill. He shouted above the noise, "Colonel, do you see those Rebels coming up the hill?"

The colonel saluted and snapped off a, "Yessir."

"I want you to take their colors. If you have to, give them the bayonet!" Colvill did what he was told and his undersized regiment

---

"Tell my wife I am shot, but we fought like Hell."

went charging into the stunned brigade from Mississippi causing my line to crumble and scatter. It cost the Minnesotans dearly though as they lost 215 men in the charge leaving only 47 men available for duty, a total of 82 percent loss.

Now I realized my planning had broken down completely. Thanks to Generals Anderson, A. P. Hill, Ewell, and even Longstreet, the trip-hammer echelon became a disjointed affair. Ewell was supposed to demonstrate when he heard the sound of Longstreet's guns. Later he said he did not hear them.

Hear them or not, at 6:30 p.m. Ewell decided to attack using Johnson's and Early's divisions, 10,000 strong. They attacked together, Johnson's troops going up Culp's Hill and Early's attacking Cemetery Hill.

Three times Johnson attacked up Culp's Hill through rocky ground and the waist deep water of Rock Creek, and three times they were driven back by General Greene's 1,310 Federals.

Early's brigades ran into Federal batteries firing on them from Culp's Hill and Cemetery Hill, and they made slow progress over the rocky ground. When they finally made it to the saddle between the hills they routed a unit of Federals at the cost of one of their best leaders, Colonel Isaac Avery. Avery was shot through the neck and fell off his horse. As he lay dying he pulled a paper and pencil out of his pocket and scribbled a note.[58] Colonel Godwin, second in command, ran over to Avery and sat down beside him. With tears in his eyes he lifted his friend's head and put it in his lap. As he stroked his hair Avery smiled up at him and gave him the note. "Give this to my father," he said, "and tell him I died facing..." A reddish bubbly froth came to his lips and his eyes closed. Avery was dead.

Godwin laid him down and jumped to his feet. "Boys," he said to the men who were crowding around their fallen leader, "let's take that hill!"

But try as they might Godwin's North Carolina men could not take the hill. For a while the North Carolinians prevailed, but then Federal reinforcements arrived and drove our men back down the slope.

---

[58] The note said: *Tell my father I died with my face to the enemy.*

Then General Hays' Louisiana Tigers found an opening and charged through. Dark had descended and visibility was limited. With a heroic Rebel Yell the Tigers took the Federal guns. When the shooting stopped, all was suddenly quiet.

In the silence that followed, General Hays could hear men talking and could see shadows, but could not tell who was approaching. Remembering Stonewall Jackson's accidental shooting, Hays told his men not to fire. But the troops were Federal and began to shoot at the Tigers. Hancock had done it again. The man leading those veteran Federal troops was Colonel Samuel Carroll a red-haired firebrand with a loud profane voice. He quickly arranged his men into battle formation and assaulted the Tigers. The Louisiana men were quickly flanked and had to scramble back down Cemetery Hill. Hancock was everywhere that day. He had won again.

That ended my battle plan for the day. The next written order I gave to the Army of Northern Virginia was:

Pull back without noise.
General Lee

It was almost 11 p.m. when I gave the final order and all we could hear now was the moans, sobs and screams of the wounded and dying. It was simply awful. Both sides under an unannounced truce went about trying to help the wounded.

Dispirited with the day's events I went to my tent. It was 2 a.m. when I awoke to a commotion outside my tent. I quickly rose in time to see the corporal-of-the-guard hustle into my tent a small, ill dressed, bearded man. It was Harrison. His first information was so accurate, I now had confidence in the former actor. I bade him to sit and asked the guard to get him some coffee, if possible.

"Thankee Gen'ral, I surely could use some."

The guard brought in two cups of chickory. I laughed to myself; *There was not one cup of coffee in the whole army, maybe the whole South, even for the commander-in-chief.*

"Well, Harrison, what have you wakened me for?"

"I wouldn't have wakened fer ye even if the Savior had come fer us. But this may be jest as important.

I wuz hangin' 'round near the Federal tent 'bout ten o'clock last night when here comes a whole gaggle uv Yankee gen'rals. Well they all strolled past the tent an' went on into the Leister house. I figgered it was important so I snuck up an' looked through a crack in the siding. Gen'ral Meade was standin' in front of the whole bunch of 'em with his spectacles on readin' some reports. The others wuz talkin to each other out loud, each one tellin' the others what they oughter do the next day.

This certainly was important, I thought. I leaned forward an' put my ear to the crack so I wouldn't miss a word.

Finally, one of the gen'rals, I think it was Butterfield, asked the others to stop their yappin' and pay attention to him. He handed each one a piece of paper. I couldn't read what it said from where I was, but luckily he read the contents out loud.

1- Should the army of the Potomac retreat or stay where it was?

2- If it did stay where it was, should it attack or stay on the defensive?

3-If the decision is to wait for an assault by Lee, how long should they wait?

All the gen'rals answers to the first question was ter stay and fight it out. The second question was answered with all the gen'rals sayin' "Stay on the defensive." The third question was answered by a variety of suggestions ranging from a few hours to a day or so.

After the gen'rals stopped talkin' they all gawked at Gen'ral Meade. He paced fer a few minutes then stopped an' turned to the other gen'rals. After a long wait he said: "The Army of the Potomac will remain in place, an' fight Lee if he attacks." The meeting was then over and the gen'rals began to leave. Gen'ral Meade stopped Gen'ral Gibbon an' quietly said to him, "Gen'ral Gibbon, if Lee attacks tomorrow it will be at your front..."

Just then I heard a noise in back of me an' I quietly left an' skedaddled over to you to give you the news."

I thanked Harrison profusely, told him his report was more valuable to me than a squad of cavalry, and told him to go find my cook, Bryan, wake him and get something to eat.

When Harrison left I began to pace the floor thinking to myself: *I was hoping Meade would leave the field, but the next morning there they will be the entire Federal Army waiting for us on the heights above Gettysburg. Well, I tried the left and right flanks and got very little success*. Then I said aloud: My men can do anything, if properly led.

I sheepishly looked around hoping no one heard me. They didn't hear a word. Everyone in the army was fast asleep except the guard marching near my tent. And he apparently hadn't heard a word.

I smiled and continued to think to myself. I have made up my mind. Tomorrow morning I will make feints on the flank and then hit the center a ferocious blow.[59]

---

[59] When the Federal meeting at the Leister House broke up, General Meade stopped General Gibbon, whose 2nd Corps held the center of the Federal line. "Gibbon," Meade said softly, "if Lee attacks tomorrow it will be on your front." "Why," a surprised Gibbon asked. "Because he has tried both flanks and failed," Meade said. "If he tries it again, it will be on our center."

I have no division now, General Lee[60]

General George Picket

Chapter 21: Gettysburg

The Third Day, July 3rd, 1863

Although he was brave, experienced and admired, there was something of the immature about General Pickett. Oh I know he quarreled with the Russians up in the Northwest and bested them, and of all things, he married a princess up there too. I also knew he shined in the Mexican war and was wounded at Gaines Mill, last year, leading a charge. But when he passed by with his hair and beard in ringlets and he smelled like a bottle of spilled perfume, well I ask you, is

---

60 After Pickett's charge failed General Lee saw Pickett riding back alone. He stopped him and said, "General Pickett you must now look to your Division." Pickett glared stonily at Lee and said, "General Lee, I have no Division now.

that the way a general in the Army of Northern Virginia should smell?[61]

On the third day of the battle of Gettysburg General Pickett was two years short of 40-years-old. Yet he was immersed in a sophomoric love affair with a teen-age Virginia beauty by the name of LaSalle Corbell. And they planned to be married right after the Gettysburg battle.

I knew none of this, and had I known I might very well have replaced Pickett in the coming assault. I wanted all my commanders to have their total mind on the business at hand.

Pickett's division was made up of Virginians. This I considered an advantage, but he had less than 6,000 men in his division and they were not veterans. Pickett's unit was formed just nine months before the battle of Gettysburg. These men also missed the Fredericksburg and Chancellorsville battles. And even when they got to Gettysburg they missed days one and two while they were detailed to watch supply wagons. That means since their inception they had had no combat

---

[61] Comments by an Army of Northern Virginia private.

experience. That worried me a bit, but Longstreet came to their support, telling me they were enthusiastic and ready to get into battle.

On July 2nd, Pickett's division marched over a large mountain to get to Gettysburg. When he got there Pickett sent word to me that his men were tired but would fight if I needed them. I wrote back the following note:

General Pickett I will not need you this evening. Let your men rest. I will let you know when I want you.
R. E. Lee, commanding

Since he had too few men in his division, my plan called for Pickett to merge with two additional divisions, one commanded by Brigadier General Johnston Pettigrew, and another by Major General Isaac Trimble. This would bring the total to 12,000 men. My prayer then, to Almighty God, was that these 12,000 Southern men and boys would bring an end to this bloody war.

I had little sleep that night and spent most of it working on a plan to defeat those people. By 5 a.m. the next morning, July 3rd, my plan was complete. It was simple. Longstreet's troops, with Pickett in the van would attack the Federal center, while Ewell would demonstrate, and then assault the Federal left.

My only concern was that Gibbon's division was in the center and Gibbon would not scare easily. On top of that the experienced and resourceful General Winfield Hancock would be in command of all the Federal forces in the center.

After a hurried breakfast, I left my tent to get things started. Just then Longstreet approached. I listened to him once more about going around the Federal left and getting into a defensive position. I guess I lost my temper. I pointed up at the Federal line on Cemetery Hill and said: "The enemy is there and I am going to strike him." After I said that there was a long silence between us.

I then told Longstreet the assault was to be made by Pickett's division along with the other two divisions I gave him. All three divisions would guide on a clump of trees near the center of the Federal line.[62] They couldn't miss the target, as the rest of Cemetery Ridge was bare of trees.

It was then that Longstreet made his final plea: "General Lee, I have been a soldier all my life. I have been with soldiers engaged in fights by couples, by squads, companies, regiments, divisions, and armies, and should know, as well as anyone what soldiers can and cannot do. It is my opinion that no 15,000 men ever arrayed for battle can take that position."

Longstreet's face fell when he saw my impatience. I turned away from him as I said, "General, I understand your concern. Please get your men ready for the charge."

I then went to inspect the men who were going to make the charge. When I got to Trimble's men I was appalled. I could see the bandages on their bodies and the exhaustion on their faces. I turned to Trimble: "General Trimble, a great many of these boys are not even fit for duty." My, God, I thought, it's too

---

[62] The target of the Confederate assault was the center of the Army of the Potomac commanded by Maj. Gen Hancock. Directly in the center was the division of Brigadier General Gibbon.

late to call this off. For their sake, this attack must succeed.

Meanwhile under orders, artillerist Colonel Porter Alexander, a hero at Fredericksburg and Chancellorsville, was placing his 75 guns to blast a path for Pickett's divisions. Eight other guns were placed to cover their flank. To back this mass of 83 guns from Longstreet's corps were A. P. Hill's 60 cannons and 24 guns of Ewell's. Now we had 167 cannons trained on the Federal line to soften them up for Pickett's charge.

While waiting for the signal to commence the bombardment Alexander got a distressing note from Longstreet that placed the decision of when Pickett should charge on Colonel Alexander.

Alexander was confused. This should not be his determination, but rather than refuse an order he sent back a note stating:

When our fire is at its best I will advise General Pickett to advance.

At precisely one o'clock the bombardment began with an ear splitting roar that seemed like it would make the earth would split apart.

For an hour and a half Alexander pounded the Yankee line until his ammunition was almost spent.

It was then that Winfield Scott Hancock showed his consummate bravery. General Hunt the head of Federal Artillery stared at Hancock as he slowly mounted his horse. Then ignoring the earthshaking bombardment, Hancock, wearing his usual snow-white shirt, and sitting ramrod straight in his saddle, rode down the line on his prancing horse. He knew how the morale of front-line troops would suffer when their officers seek shelter in the rear.

The Federal soldiers on the line gawked and gaped at Hancock as the general and a lone orderly, holding the corps flag, sauntered by them while 167 Confederate guns lofted shell after shell tearing up the ground around the serene Hancock and that lonesome, frightened orderly.

When Hancock reached the middle of the Federal line an unnamed brigadier jumped out of the line and confronted Hancock: "General," he said emphatically, "the corps commander ought not risk his life this way."

Hancock smiled and replied: “There are times when a corps commander’s life doesn’t count very much.” After that confrontation Hancock continued, unhurt, to the end of the line and dismounted to the cheers of the entire Union army.

Unknown to us, most of Alexander’s shells were too high and only the Federal rear guard suffered from the shelling. General Meade’s headquarters was hit wounding General Butterfield and killing an orderly, who was serving the generals their lunch. Also 16 Federal horses were decimated.

Amazingly the Federal line just behind the stone wall was virtually untouched. Meade and his aides quickly moved back to a safer location.

However Alexander’s guns had zeroed in on the Federal guns behind the angle led by a Major Brown. With most of his gunners dead and his cannons destroyed Major Brown began to pull his damaged guns back off the line.

At that moment Major Osborne, watching the cannons being withdrawn approached General Hunt. “It occurred to me,” Osborn said, “that General Meade might want Lee to attack him.”

Hunt nodded his head in the affirmative. "I actually heard him say just that."

"If that's the case I would cease fire at once. Then the enemy could reach only one conclusion and that is that we have been driven from this hill."

General Hunt's eyes lit up. "Major, you're right, I will attend to it at once."

General Hunt immediately gave the order to his gunners to stop firing and save their ammunition for the Confederate charge he was sure would come. He then went over to Major Brown and told him to make a big show of pulling his smashed guns off the line.

Of course, we knew nothing of this exchange except that the Federal fire slowed considerably. When he observed the slowdown, Colonel Alexander picked up his binoculars and surveyed the Federal line scanning slowly from left to right. As the Federal fire died down to a sporadic, desultory bombardment Alexander came upon the sight of Major Brown frantically pulling back his guns. Alexander looked to the heavens, pumped his fist and muttered, "Thank you God."

To be absolutely sure, he put his binoculars back to his eyes. What he saw was

Cushing also pulling his damaged guns off the line. That was enough for Alexander and he quickly wrote a note to General Pickett:

The Federal guns have been driven off. For God's sake, come quick, or we cannot support you. Our ammunition is almost gone.

Alexander

As he was writing the note to Pickett, Alexander did not notice Federal Captain Andrew Cowan bringing up new cannons to replace Brown's damaged ones. In Cushing's case, he was merely exchanging his cannons for others that would fire canister accurately.

Pickett got Alexander's message, but instead of a jubilant general ready to lead his troops to glory, I noticed General Pickett was quiet and thoughtful.

Off to his left was Brigadier James Kemper who had been fighting the Yankees since Bull Run. Next to him just mounting his black charger was Brigadier General Richard Garnett. Garnett should have not been on a horse when he led his men in the Gettysburg charge but he thought he had something to prove. I told him I had forbidden officers who were leading men to conduct themselves on horseback, but this is what he told me: "General Lee, yesterday I was kicked by my horse and severely injured. I can barely walk so I must ride to lead my men."

"But General Garnett if you ride in the charge you will be an easy target..."

"General Lee, as you already know, last year, Turner Ashby rode into camp and reported to Stonewall Jackson that General Shields had four Union regiments in our rear, about the same size as our little army. Jackson immediately ordered me to attack them. Unfortunately, Ashby was in error about their size. Shields had a full Infantry Division, 9,000 men which was twice the size of Jackson's force. Regardless of their size, orders are orders, so I made the attack. I was soon outgunned and surrounded so I made the best of the situation and retreated. When I got back Jackson was furious and called me a coward. Infuriated myself, I challenged him to a duel, but he had me arrested and charged me with, "neglect of duty." My court martial started in August with only Jackson testifying.

But the trial was suspended by you General Lee, as you wanted me along at the second Bull Run battle (in September, 1862.) Jackson may be dead but I have been called a coward and I must make the assault, horse or no horse, to refute this charge against me. And since my horse wounded me yesterday it will be, on my horse."

What could I say to that? When honor is at stake it's best to stay silent.

Meanwhile Pickett's men were ordered to huddle behind low breastworks and fence rails on the slant of Cemetery Ridge.

Meanwhile Hancock was sure that morale of the Federal men would be improved if their artillery answered the Rebel barrage. So, ignoring General Hunt's entreaty to halt the bombardment, the Federal guns under Hancock's control, on Cemetery Hill, began firing at the west slope of Seminary Ridge. Pickett's men paid the price. Since the Confederate troops were lying close together, in the 90 degree heat[63], single shells would

---

[63] It was, one professor said, 87 degrees on the afternoon of Pickett's charge. The humidity was smothering and some of the Union soldiers waiting for the charge even fell asleep.

land among them and kill and wound 4 or 5 at a time, even up to ten. Before Pickett's men staged for the assault, 500 of them would never fight again.

Carrying Alexander's note, Pickett rode over to Longstreet who was absently whittling on a piece of wood.

"General," Picket asked quietly, "Alexander says it's time. Shall I advance?"

A morose Longstreet never answered but did bow his head.

Assuming the affirmative Pickett snapped a salute and said: I shall lead my division forward, sir."

As he turned to go back to his men Cadmus Wilcox offered him his flask. "Pickett, take a drink with me."

"Cadmus, I cannot. I promised LaSalle..."

Cadmus interrupted, "But Pickett, in an hour you'll be in hell or glory."

Pickett shook his head and cantered up to the head of the three divisions. After a few moments he turned to his men, and in a sergeant's voice he said clearly, "Charge the enemy and remember *Old Virginia!"* Picket then turned his horse around and faced toward the Federal army, a mile away. He put his fist in the air and roared, "Forwarrrrrrd! Guide center! Maaarrrrch!"

I always thought the Yankees had something to do with the defeat

---

General George Pickett

Chapter 22: Pickett's Charge

July 3rd 1863 The Third Day

Time was heavy for the Federal soldiers on Cemetery Hill and many of them were at rest in the copse of trees and behind the stone wall. All at once the sky suddenly turned the color of brass and the air was filled with murderous iron again. It was 2:30 p.m. and Porter Alexander had just restarted his bombardment.

A short while before the second shelling began I had a meeting with General Stuart. I told him: "I will send you a semaphore signal that General Pickett was moving out to charge the Federal line. I want you then to line up your four brigades, all 6,300 men, on the plain at Hanover Road, and then strike the rear of the Federal Line. When you strike the back of their line, the Yankees would have to deal with us at their front and rear."

When his men were lined up properly Stuart faced them toward the rear of the Federal line. When the semaphore flag dropped signifying Pickett's charge, Stuart shouted: "Ready, men! For General Lee and the Old South, CHAAAARRRRGE!"

With that stirring call to arms Stuart's divisions leaped into action. But the Federal Cavalry, led by George Custer, was waiting for them.

Charge and counter charge by both sides was the order of the day and to Stuart's frustration they were evenly matched.

Knowing Pickett was counting on him striking the Federal rear, Stuart had enough of the standoff and he called in his heavy hitters, Wade Hampton's and Fitzhugh Lee's brigades.

Preparing for their charge, their precision all but awed the enemy. But it wasn't enough. When Hampton and Lee charged they met a full measure of shot and shell that tore great holes in their formations. Still they came on.

From the opposite direction, General George Custer leading the 1st Michigan bravely dashed headlong into the two Confederate brigades shouting, “Come on, you Wolverines!”

When the two columns came together it was like the crash of two maddened bulls on a narrow mountain road. So violent was the collision that men were unseated by the crash and thrown to the ground only to be crushed by wildly careening horses.

As the fierce sword and handgun fight ensued, both Rebel flanks were attacked by another Federal cavalry unit, led by the 3rd Pennsylvania. With both their front and flanks attacked and with Federal artillery lobbing shells at them the Confederates soon gave way and retreated to Cress’s Ridge.

Both sides claimed victory, but I knew who won. The rear of the Federal line was still intact.

A very proud Union Cavalry man said it best, “We saved the day at the most critical moment of the Battle of Gettysburg.”

Of course I had no way of knowing what had happened to Stuart and was concentrating on Pickett and his men.

George Pickett

I have no division now, General Lee

Alexander must give you the order to charge for I can't

General Longstreet

Chapter 23: Out of the Woods into Hell

Three of my divisions led by George Pickett now marched out of the woods where they had staged and moved toward death and glory.

Both sides had now silenced their guns and my men marched at the steady pace of 100 yards per minute.

In the distance on both Little and Big Round Tops, I saw Federal semaphore men counting the blue battle flags of Pickett and the red ones of Trimble and Pettigrew. That would tell them how many men I had in the charge, and of course, they would forward that information to General Meade.

I dropped my binoculars down to my own men.

Longstreet was whittling as usual. I wished he had been more enthusiastic about my plan. It might have made some difference.

I moved my binoculars forward. There was Kemper, steady reliable Kemper in front of his men marching with them at 100 yards per minute.

I moved my binoculars to the left. General Garnett was leaning forward on his horse examining the terrain at his front. Oh I hope he survives. But on horseback? How could he? Well, I don't give him much of a chance but I will pray for him. It pains me to think it, but he didn't deserve the stigma Jackson gave him.

Ah, and here is Armistead, as brave as any man waving his sword with his hat perched on it.

Where is Pickett? Ah, yes there he is, 20 yards to the rear, just where the commander should be.

My eyes surveyed the marching men in the ranks dressed in gray, butternut and homespun. God willing they should have been dressed in gold.

Now Pickett's men are out of the woods. They get an order to close with Pettigrew's men. The Federal guns are very accurate and several of my soldiers are killed with each shell. It's almost too hard to watch. But wait, they have reached a dip in the ground that gives them at least a bit of cover. But men are still being hit behind them as they halt and awe, everyone watching as they close the gaps caused by the bombing and re-dress their lines.

Oh, no! Look at this. It's Mayo's brigade. They're late coming out of the woods and they're double-timing to catch up. What's this! They are stopping and... Good God, that's a skirmish line of Ohioans. They are firing into Mayo's boys. REFUSE THE LINE COLONEL MAYO AND TURN YOUR MEN TOWARD THE SKIRMISHERS!

Oh no! Mayo's men are running. Thank God the other men are far in front of them and can't see this disgraceful retreat.

A.P. Hill

A fine General who displayed excellent skill in his later battles

Home, boys, home! Over that hill is home!

Louis Addison Amistead

Chapter 24: Pickett's Charge

At first, flags whipping in the 90 degree heat, Pickett led his men toward the Federal line. Then, gradually he dropped back to 20 yards behind the three divisions.

Following, Pickett's lead brigade in the silence that prevailed when the bombing ceased, was Richard Garnett on his coal black stallion, sitting firm in his saddle, eyes on the prize that was the copse of trees a mile ahead.

Following behind Garnett's brigade was General Lewis Armistead heading toward his closest friend, Winfield Scott Hancock who was in charge of the center defense of the Federal line. In his pocket was a gift for his dearest friend, Hancock, his personal watch he wanted Hancock to have if he failed the charge.

Brigadier General Armistead advanced on foot and as he advanced pulled his sword out of its scabbard, put his black slouch hat on the tip and waved it above his head so his troops could see it. Shouting to his men to keep up, he quickened his steps his eyes fixed on the Stone Wall and his heart on his friend, Hancock.

Watching the awesome display coming right at him was General Hays who was not one bit perturbed by the display. He was a rare soldier who loved mortal combat and couldn't wait for the Rebels to come. While he was waiting he had his men perform a brisk drill to keep their minds off the coming fight. When they were done he had his men drop behind the Stone Wall and dig in.

Watching the breathtaking advance of the Confederate army, Union men with shaking hands put Minié balls and bayonets in and on their gun barrels. Gunners loaded shells in their cannons, gripped their lanyards and prepared to light their fuses. Artillerists led by Major Alonzo Cushing in the front line had his men load their guns with canister to decimate any soldier who dared to try to get over the Stone Wall.[64]

The silence was suddenly broken with a Federal bombardment from six parrots on Little Round Top and McGilvery's guns on Cemetery Ridge. According to Major Charles Payton of Virginia, "They could not miss. The Federal cannons fired with lethal effect, sometimes as many as ten men being killed and wounded by one shell.

With an awesome display of courage the Rebel force closed the gaps, caused by the murderous bombs, redressed their lines and started forward again.

Now Pettigrew and Pickett have joined and without stopping are maintaining their steady pace. They have still not fired a shot and now they have reached the last hill, a slow rise to the wall and the copse of trees. I see General Armistead turn his back to the Federal line and address his troops. I found out later what he said to them:

---

[64] Major Alonzo Cushing was promoted to Lt. Colonel posthumously as a result of his gallantry on July 3rd 1863. In 2010, after a lengthy investigation started in 2002, Congress ordered that Colonel Cushing be awarded the Medal of Honor.

"Home boys, home! Remember, home is over beyond that hill!"

I moved my binoculars to our front lines approaching the stone wall. My stomach turns as I see the Federal Guns decimating my boys at the center. On the right, my troops reach a pair of sturdy rail fences 200 yards from the wall and begin to climb over them. I almost turn away. It's painful to see those brave boys fall from the accurate fire of fifteen hundred muskets and ten cannons. As far away from them as I am I hear a ghastly moan. It's too much and I do turn away with tears in my eyes.

After a few moments I put the binoculars back to my eyes and I see Colonel Marshall fall from his horse and then Pettigrew go down. But wait, there is Colonel Fry crossing over the wall with the battle flag. Maybe all is not lost. But then I see the Federals flanking Pettigrew's troops. Those poor boys…

Now it was Kemper's turn. Federal troops from Vermont had flanked him and were now pouring lethal fire into his flank forcing Kemper's men to veer to their left into the brigades of Garnett and Armistead. I see Kemper trying to realign them yelling, "Go for their guns, boys," when he is shot by a sniper.[65]

Now the Federal fire is coming from both flanks and the boys stop going forward and try to escape the bullets. This leads to mass commotion. I see Garnett trying to straighten things out when he simply disappears from sight. I try to turn away again but cannot. Oh, wait there is Garnett at the stone wall. He is waving his men on to cross over... He disappears again... Oh God, there is his black charger racing back to our lines. The horse is covered with blood. I hang my head. Poor Garnett.[66]

I look up in time to see Pickett's division is now directly in front of the stone wall. "Go, you Virginians, go." I only wish I could join them.

I shake my head. As brave as they are, they are taking a terrible beating from the Federal artillery, firing canister at them from point blank range. It's almost too much to

---

65 The bullet strikes near Kemper's spine leaving him partially paralyzed.

66 Garnett was never seen again. Years later his battle sword was found in a Baltimore second hand shop by ex-General Maryland Steuart. How it got there is a mystery.

bear, but bear it I will. Ho, what's this? Armistead is on top of the wall. Dare I hope? Yes, the Federal gunners are retreating. And here comes Armistead. He's over the wall with his hat now halfway down his sword as he turns back to his men, "Come on, boys give them the cold steel," he yells, "who will follow me?" He reaches for a cannon, puts his hand on it and falls, mortally wounded by a Minié ball.[67] But before he falls his men have heard him and they swarm over the wall.

Hancock is warned by an alert, Colonel Devereux that the Rebel troops have broken through the Federal defense and are over the wall.

Hancock responds. "Plug that hole Devereux, pretty God-damned quick."

Devereux orders his men into the charging Rebels and the two lines come together with a colossal shudder that stops them both. The lines rebound from the shock and when they

---

[67] Armistead asked to be brought to his friend, Hancock. When he heard Hancock was wounded also, but not mortally, he gave his watch to a Federal officer to give to Hancock and his bible to be given to Hancock's wife, Almira. He died speaking about Almira singing, Colleen Malvoreen at a dinner he never forgot.

recover they begin killing each other, blindly and without mercy.

Stepping over the dead and wounded both lines, standing toe to toe, fighting with pistols, rifles, knives, and fists screaming oaths and yells they kill, and kill, and kill and die.

For the men at the wall the sun stands still. The soldiers feel like they have always been here, right in this place, killing and being killed.

But finally it's over. Every one of the Rebels who got over the wall is dead, wounded or captured.

Snarling at the Yankees standing their ground the surviving Confederates slowly, reluctantly, begin to retreat ebbing back down the slope of Cemetery Hill toward their own lines.

I have failed them and now I begin to wish I were with the glorious dead on that stone wall.

I see the Federal officers trying to rally their men to pursue the retreating Confederates but the soldiers are wiser than the officers as I would have prepared a wall of fire to greet them they would not soon forget.[68]

As if in a last retribution, while my boys are retreating, the two Federals who were the architects of the Confederate defeat are struck down. Gibbon, who was instrumental in staving off defeat in the middle and Hancock who was the master of the entire central defense are both wounded.[69]

As the men come trudging back from their forlorn attempt to breech the Federal line, I greet them the best I know how saying, "Don't despair! It's all my fault! Go back and fall into line. We must prepare for an attack by those people. It's all my fault."

I looked up the hill to the Codori Farm. There is Pickett still on his horse, his head down. After a few moments he turned his horse and follows his men back to our lines. When he reached me I said, "General Pickett,

---

[68] For Meade not to expect that Lee would not have a plan to have cleared fields of fire and a massive retaliation for a Federal charge would have been foolish in the extreme.

[69] Gibbon suffered a shoulder wound and had to leave the field. Hancock, while guiding the defense was badly wounded when a Minié ball struck his saddle and drove splinters and a nail into his thigh. When he saw the nail he said, "They must be hard-up for ammunition."

it's all my fault, but you must now look to your men. You must get your division ready to repel a Federal attack."

Pickett looked down on me from horseback and said coldly, "General Lee, I have no division now!"

As much as I hated to admit it, he was very nearly speaking the truth. Of the 6,000 men he started out with he had lost, by a later count, 3,000 of them. I let him pass without another word.

I spent the rest of the day getting the men in a defensive position to resist any attack by the Federal army. But as I said before, Meade will commit no blunder in my front, and if I make one, he will make haste to take advantage of it. He would not do what the fools did at Fredericksburg and Chancellorsville.

Despite my wishing he would attack he did not do so and the next day both armies spent the rest of the day glaring at each other while licking their wounds.

Then, as happened so often in this war, the skies opened up and a deluge swept the ground. It was as if God himself was trying to clean the earth of the blood we had spilled there.

That evening at our hospital tent, I turned to Taylor and said, "We have had too many casualties and have too little ammunition left. We must now return to Virginia."

But saying is not doing, so I spent the rest of the day at my tent, pouring over maps, by candlelight, to find the best way home. I knew that General Imboden's fresh cavalry brigade had arrived at Gettysburg that afternoon and I sent a courier to have him meet me at headquarters tent. When I got to the tent I was weary to the bone.

But let me here have Imboden himself tell you what he wrote about what he saw and heard:

General Lee arrived at his headquarters tent between one and two in the morning. It was a good thing Traveller knew the way there, as General Lee was lost in thought and oblivious as to where he was. The horse stopped in front of the tent and Lee just sat there motionless. Finally he began to dismount. He threw his right leg over the back of the saddle and was so exhausted he simply slid down the side of the horse. I rushed to grab him but he hit the ground squarely and held me off with his right hand. The moon shown full and revealed an expression of great sadness on his face. Both his hands trembled and there were tears in his eyes. All I could think of to say was, "General, this has been a hard day for you."

He shook his massive head and said: "Yes, it has been a sad, sad day for us." Then he stood there for a minute or two, leaning on Traveller, took a deep breath and said with endless remorse, "Too bad. Too bad. Oh! TOO BAD!"

John D. Imboden

There's the Devil to pay

General John Buford, Jr.

Chapter 25: Retreat to Virginia

That night I outlined the difficult task of transporting the wounded and the supplies to Imboden. I knew it would be dangerous because the enemy cavalry was nearby and we might have to deal with civilian spies along the way. Worst of all, when they find we are gone, the Federal divisions might come alive and come after us.

The trip back with the wagons loaded with wounded was a nightmare. Many of the wounded died on the way and the roads were so rough the ones who didn't die kept wishing they would.

But the boys still had lots of fight in them. I heard one soldier on the march say to another: "What if the Yanks come?" The other one answered: We'll fight them 'til hell freezes over, and then we'll fight them on the ice." And fight they did because Meade's cavalry struck at us every time they could.

Even the Gettysburg civilians got into the act of vengeance. Late in the day they came at us with axes and cut the wheels of many of our wagons leaving them unusable. The civilians were quickly chased away by our cavalry.

On the morning of July 7th, we finally reached the Potomac River. To our consternation it was too high to cross but Imboden had found some flatboats. It could only carry a few persons at a time so I had the men dig in and I ordered my engineers to build a pontoon bridge. What they did build was a shaky, but usable bridge. They built it just in time as the expected Federal infantry attack finally came.

I lost many men, dead at the Potomac River, and 1,500 men who were covering our retreat were captured, but their bravery let us escape to fight again.

His Excellency Jefferson Davis
Headquarters Army of Northern Virginia Near the Potomac River, Penn., July 5th, 1863

Mr. President:

My letter of yesterday informed you of the disposition of this army. Though reduced in numbers due to the hardship and battles through which it has passed its condition is good and its confidence unimpaired. We are now being trailed by Federal cavalry and since we cannot cross the river into Virginia because of heavy rains I may have to do battle once more.

I hope your Excellency will understand that I am not in the least discouraged and that my faith in the All Merciful God is still strong while the fortitude of this army is equally robust.

I am conscious that the enemy has been much shattered in the recent battle as we have too. But I am also aware that he can be easily reinforced while few additional numbers can be added to my army.

General Barksdale is killed. Generals Garnett and Armistead are missing, and I am told one of them is dead and the other wounded and a prisoner. Pender and Trimble have leg wounds and Hood a severe arm wound. General Kemper is mortally wounded and General Wade Hampton is also wounded but in a different battle.

Very respectfully, your obedient servant,

R. E. Lee, Gen'l Commanding

The art of war is simple. Find your enemy and get him

Ulysses S. Grant

Chapter 26: A Thorny Problem

Just as Grant took command of the Federal Armies, a matter of importance came to a head in both Washington and Richmond. When I heard of it I was as horrified as the northern population.

It seems that the northern government got incensed when they learned our government was sending Negro soldiers not to prisons, but back to their former masters.

Secretary-of-War Stanton, who championed the "no exchange of prisoners", told Grant that to exchange the men but exclude the black soldiers and their officers was to abandon the negroes and their commanders to Southern slavers.

In addition, when escaped Federal soldiers came north and told of the bestial conditions the captured soldiers lived in at places like Andersonville and Libby Prison, the Federal army, officers and men, became as angry as disturbed swarms of wasps.

Escaped soldiers, looking like starving, skeletal men, said that Federal soldiers who became prisoners were being sent to Southern prison camps and were starving, and dying at an extraordinary rate.

Northern newspapermen got wind of the prison camp horrors, printed pictures of the living skeletons, and their newspapers began to spread the word to the Northern civilians.

Horrified, Northerners began to put pressure on their congressmen to restart the exchange of prisoners.

Personally, I was against the policy of the South regarding captured Negro troops. Up to this time, throughout the war, both sides had been periodically exchanging captured men on an even exchange, man for man. But when the South refused to recognize escaped slaves in Federal uniforms as Federal soldiers, and had sent them back to their former masters in servitude, the deal of exchange quickly unraveled. On top of that, the white officers who led the black soldiers were considered criminals by the Confederacy and were made liable, under southern state laws for fueling slave uprisings. Anxious to get our veterans back again I wrote to Grant and proposed the following:

General Grant:
I propose that the armies in Virginia go back to the original exchange of prisoners on a straight man-to-man basis.

Grant wrote back:

General Lee:
Among those lost by the armies operating against Richmond were a number of colored troops. Before further negotiations are had upon the subject I would ask if you propose delivering these men the same as white soldiers?

I answered reluctantly:

General Grant:
Deserters from my army and Negroes belonging to our citizens are not considered subjects for exchange, and were not included in my proposition..."

Grant's answer was succinct:

General Lee:
"The Northern government is bound to secure to all soldiers received into her armies the rights due to soldiers.
The deal is off.
Gen'l Grant

By then the new commander of the Union Armies, Ulysses Grant, was called in by Secretary Stanton and told of the prisoner conditions and the civilian concerns. Grant agreed with their concerns but not with their conclusions.

To state his position clearly he wrote the following letter to General Butler, the general in charge of prisoner exchange:

General Butler:
It is hard on our men held in Southern prisons not to be exchanged, but it is humane to those left in the ranks to fight our battles.
Every man we hold as a prisoner, when released on parole or otherwise, becomes an active soldier against us at once, either directly or indirectly.
If we commence a system of exchange that liberates all prisoners taken, we will have to fight on until the whole South is exterminated. If we hold those captured then they amount to no more than one more dead man.
At this particular time to release all Rebel prisoners it could insure Sherman's defeat and would compromise the position of the Army of the Potomac.
Ulysses S. Grant, Lt. General

General Butler later found out that we had put the captured Negroes to work at Fort Gilmer. In retaliation, he took the same amount of white Southern soldiers out of prison and put them to work digging trenches on the front line.

When I found that Beast Butler had done this, I recanted the order and put the Negroes back in prison.

Grant responded by telling Butler to do the same and sent me a note:

General Lee:
As painful as it may be to me, if treatment of Federal prisoners is not properly accorded, then I shall inflict the same treatment on a like number of Confederate prisoners.
Gen'l Grant

Actually, the South hoped to gain a great deal from the Federal Army's refusal to exchange prisoners. The Federal war department had been getting petitions from the prisoners at Andersonville, begging that exchanges be made. The Southern congress even went to the extreme of combing the prison camps to find anti-Lincoln men and paroling them to tell the population about the no exchange policy, and to vote against Lincoln in the upcoming election. And the voting was to be held in the Federal Army as well as the civilian population.

The South knew that the men of the Army of the Potomac disliked many of their generals and had most likely forgotten what he was fighting for in the first place.

Knowing that the South might be right there was talk in Washington about denying the right of the vote to the soldiers.

Grant's answer to Secretary-of-War Stanton was a ringing affirmation for the democratic process and made me ashamed of our own position. The following is Grant's letter to Stanton:

Secretary Stanton:
The exercise of the right to vote by the officers and soldiers of the armies in the field is a novel thing. It has generally been considered dangerous

to constitutional liberty and subversive of military discipline. But our circumstances are novel. A large part of our legal voters are now under arms, or otherwise engaged in military service of the United States. Most of these men are not regular soldiers, nor are they mercenaries who give their services to the government for pay and have no interest in the political questions involved. On the contrary they are American citizens having their homes, social and political ties binding them to their states from which they come and to which they will return.

The have left their homes temporarily to sustain their country in its hour of trial. In performing this sacred duty they should not be deprived of a most precious privilege. They have as much right to demand that their votes shall be counted in the choice of their rulers

as the citizens who remain at home. Nay, more, for these men have sacrificed more for their country than any civilian.
I state these reasons in full, for the unusual thing of allowing armies in the field to vote and be given the nothing more than the fullest right of that exercise.[70]

Ulysses S. Grant

****

When we reached Richmond, I set about resting and refitting my army. Then after much deliberation I sent for General Early. I sat him down and told him something he already knew. My army was starving and living on green apples and stunted corn.

He asked, "General Lee, what can I do to help."

---

[70] Sheridan had been winning stunning victories in the Shenandoah and Sherman was equally successful. It was now obvious that the soldiers would not vote themselves out of the war as they were finally winning it.

I then asked him if he would take his men and help me save the army. He answered, "Yes."

I spent the rest of the day giving General Early two tasks.

The next morning General Jubal Early began to move down the Shenandoah Valley in hopes of saving the South's breadbasket.

My hope was by sending General Early toward Washington, by way of the Shenandoah was to make General Grant take men from his army to deal with Early and thereby relieve the pressure on my army. I reinforced Early by sending him Kershaw's division along with a brigade of cavalry.

The Yankees knew something was up and General Sheridan shadowed Early almost as soon as he left Richmond. By mid-October both armies were shadowing each other near Cedar Creek, Virginia.

While he was near Washington, Sheridan had received a request from General Halleck to come to there on important business. Sheridan immediately left to confer with General Halleck, leaving his second in command of his troops at Cedar Creek.

Thinking his men could deal with anything Early could throw at them Sheridan felt secure leaving them with a subordinate.

To trick the Federal army, Early had his signalmen send a fake message from Longstreet to Early saying Longstreet was on his way to join Early to destroy Sheridan's army.

Early knew there was no good area for Sheridan to retreat to and hoped that when he got the message he would retreat all the way back to the Potomac.

The message was copied by the deluded signalmen but the Federals would not retreat and the battle was on.

Sheridan was not at Cedar Creek and Early found it easy going against the Federals without Sheridan.

But Sheridan was not too far off. He was on his way back to his army after spending the night in Winchester. When he woke that morning he immediately started toward his camp. When he got to a few miles from his campground he heard gunfire and was puzzled and a bit nervous. He urged his mount, Rienzi to a full gallop toward the noise. He soon came upon a road clogged with defeated Union soldiers.

At dawn, Early had struck the leaderless Federal army in front and flank and had driven it back in a rout.

When Sheridan arrived he found his men in disarray and the Rebels looting his camp.

Screaming at the top of his lungs, Sheridan got his men back in line and counter attacked the now disorganized Rebel Army.

No one could lead men in battle like Sheridan. Before the Rebel army could reorganize they were in headlong flight away from Cedar Creek, with the Federal Army at their heels urged on by a madman on a fiery black horse and a voice that would wake the dead. In a short while the battle was over.

That ended all hope of saving our breadbasket and upsetting the government in Washington. In fact the routing of Early's army helped Lincoln get reelected.

Sheridan's message after the battle was brief and to the point:

At first affairs looked bleak, but by the gallantry of our brave men and officers, disaster had been converted to a splendid victory. Only darkness saved Early's army from complete destruction.

I will allow you no other terms than unconditional and immediate surrender

---

Ulysses S. Grant

Chapter 27: The Wilderness[71] May 5-7, 1864

In late April, 1864, as I was going over some correspondence from Richmond, there were suddenly several loud voices issuing demands outside my tent.

I looked over at Major Veneble and he shrugged his shoulders. "Major," I said quietly to him, "would you kindly see what the ruckus outside is all about."

The major got up but before he could take a step the tent flap opened and the corporal

---

[71] The Wilderness is a jungle of second-growth timber with few clearings and vine covered trails. It's a region of scrub growth and stunted timber that's hard to fight in and worse for maneuvering. It extends 15 miles from east to west and 10 miles from north to south.

who was walking guard entered with his left hand holding his rifle and his right circled around the neck of a raggedly dressed civilian. Just behind them was the Officer of the day. I immediately recognized the poorly dressed scout, Harrison.

"Gen'ral, tell this no'count baboon ter let go uv me or ah'll...

"Let him go corporal, believe it or not he's one of my... er General Longstreet's scouts."

"Yessir General, I only thought..."

The officer of the day spoke up. "It's alright Corporal, you can leave.

The Corporal cocked his head, shrugged his shoulders, and said, "Yessir." He saluted me and was gone. The officer also saluted, said, "Sorry, sir," and quickly left.

An indignant Harrison muttered, "Well, I never..."

"Major, please get a notebook and jot down what you hear." I then turned to Harrison.

"Harrison twice you gave me information that was very timely. What have you got for me this time?"

"Gen'ral I got some mighty important news fer ya, but I'm starved. Ya think I kin get some grub?"

I looked over to Veneble. “Major take care of that for our guest. And, oh yes, bring him an after dinner cigar.” Then I smiled and added, “But don’t wrap any orders around the cigars.

Veneble laughed as he left the tent.

“Orders? Cigars?...

I turned back to the scout. “It’s a private joke, Harrison. Now, give me the latest information. General Longstreet will see that you’re paid.”

“I preciate that Gen’ral but in Yankee gold please. I cain’t use Rebel script no more no how.”

I smiled at him and said, “Continue.”

Harrison leaned forward and in a whisper began to speak. “Gen’ral a few days ago President Lincoln promoted that there Gen’ral Useless Grant up to Lieutenant General an’ give him command uv all the Union Armies.”

I shook my head. Harrison waited for a few moments and then continued. “The strange thing is Grant chose to make his headquarters with the Army of the Potomac.”

“Meade is gone? I asked.”

"No," Harrison answered with a grin, "as I said, that's the strange part, Meade stays where he was, commanding the Army of the Potomac, an' Sherman takes over for Grant in the west. One more thing, Gen'ral. On May 4th, Grant crossed the Rapidan River and headed for Wilderness Tavern. If'n you hurry you kin head him off like y'all did Hooker a while back.

I knew when I read about the surrender demand by General Grant, before the capitulation of Fort Donelson, that he would be a competent and dangerous opponent. I needed to know more.[72] "Harrison, tell me about this fellow, Grant."

"Well, Gen'ral he's a westerner, Ohio man I think, kinda stoic an' solid. He dresses seedy-like, an' he's as plain as a field of corn in the mid-west heat. Unpretentious is what I mean. But no matter how he looks, when he starts out fer somethin' you jes know he

---

[72] Gen. Buckner, Yours of this date, proposing armistice and appointment of commissioners to settle terms of capitulation, is just received. No terms other than unconditional and immediate surrender can be accepted. I propose to move immediately upon your works.

Gen. U. S. Grant.

means ter get it.[73] Oh, an' somethin' else, he rides a big bay called *Cincinnati,* an' if you git a chance, you'd best shoot him off thet horse."

Veneble entered the tent and I signaled to him. He motioned to Harrison then turned to me. "General, if you're through with this, er, scout, I'll take him for dinner."

I returned Harrison's goodbye salute and the two men slipped out of the tent.

Pondering the situation of a new Federal commander, I pulled out the maps and spread them out on the table. *H'mmm*, I said to myself, *if I were Grant the last thing I would want to do is fight in the Wilderness.*

Veneble came back into the tent and stood quietly waiting for instructions. I looked up from the map and said, "Major Veneble, get Major Taylor, we need to modify our strategy for the Wilderness."

---

[73] General Longstreet said of Grant, "That man will fight us every day and every hour until the end of the war.

Phillip Sheridan

If I owned Texas and Hell, I would rent out Texas and live in Hell

It was as though Christian men had turned into fiends residing in the bottom of hell

Colonel Horace Porter

Chapter 28: A Night to Remember

I finished redeploying my troops in the Wilderness on May 4th. While they dug in I stood on the bank of the Rapidan River and stared into the blackness of the medieval forest, the Wilderness. I knew it was a forest of death because of the previous battle we had fought in the Wilderness was at the Battle of Chancellorsville where so many men died. Some of the men killed in the Wilderness still lay unburied. I had no illusions about this horrid place. If someone cupped his ear and listened carefully they could almost still hear the cries of the wounded who could not escape the flames caused by the weapons of the two armies.

I looked carefully around me with an engineer's eye. The thickly wooded trees in the Wilderness stand very close together, and their branches will allow no sunshine to reach the ground. And where the sun did manage to filter through it nourished stunted pines and tough, dense, gnarly underbrush that grew everywhere not allowing a path or trail where a man might walk unimpeded. Vines, and creepers like massive green spider webs laced themselves around the disorderly growing trees making visibility over a few yards a difficult sighting for a rifleman.

To make things worse for the men who would fight there, small, black, sunless streams crisscrossed the entire Wilderness making the ground a soggy, swampy, shoe-sucking morass, hard to walk on and worse to march on. It was probably the very last place on earth that either army would pick to make a fight.

I heard one of my men telling a Federal prisoner: "When your cavalry crossed the Rapidan we yelled out to y'all, 'Where y'all goin'. 'And your cavalry would yell back,' "On to Richmond." Then we would say: Y'all better hope Bobby Lee has nuthin' ter say about that.'[74]

I sure hope my boys are right. This fellow Grant has a lot more men then we do, and an endless amount of supplies. But this African forest I see in front of me is a great equalizer, and I will have lots to say about those Federals coming over this twelve by six miles of wasteland.

The first day the Federals crossed the Rapidan our cavalry watched them as best they could. But no one interfered with them as I ordered that they were not to be molested until I gave the command.

The Federals marched deeper into the Wilderness until they reached the abandoned Wilderness Tavern. The Tavern itself had no significance except at the Battle of Chancellorsville we had a field hospital in back of the Tavern where General Jackson's arm was amputated.

A short distance from the Tavern were two roads that would figure greatly in the

---

[74] A reporter asked General Grant, "How long will it take you to get to Richmond. Grant answered, "Four days. That is if General Lee becomes a party to the agreement. If he objects the trip might take longer."

battle to come. They were, the Orange Turnpike and the Orange Plank Road. The Orange Plank Road led out of the Wilderness.

All through the night of May 4th there was an ominous rumbling from the west. This was created by my order to move the army south to get between Richmond and the Federals.

That night was difficult for both armies, but worse for those people as we had some idea of the terrain, while they had little. Also Hancock's men had camped on an old Chancellorsville battlefield and they kept turning up bleached bones and skulls. Many a Yankee in Hancock's corps had a sleepless time that night.

The next morning the Federals started marching south. I then ordered A. P. Hill and Richard Ewell, and their men, to meet and stop them.

Spring had come and with it the two old adversaries closed in on each other for one more battle.

The Federals crossed the Rapidan and Germanna and Ely's Fords led by Hancock, Gouverneur Warren and Ambrose Burnside. Burnside had fallen in favor because of his failed strategy at Fredericksburg and gained it back again with his successful defense of Knoxville. But he will lose it once more at the Wilderness.

My scouts soon confirmed my prediction of the Ely and Germanna fordings by the Federals, and I quickly became aware of the movement of those people and acted to counter them. In my heart I knew this battle might be the glorious beginning of the Confederacy or its ignoble end. Last evening I wrote in my journal:

If victorious, we have everything to live for. If defeated, there will be nothing left to live for.

Ulysses S. Grant

I propose to fight it out on this line if it takes all summer

I hate war as only a soldier who has lived it can

An American Soldier

Chapter 29: Ulysses Grant

This book would not be complete without a chapter on my old enemy, and now friend, President Ulysses Grant.

When we met at the surrender at Appomattox, I could not recall General Grant. But as the negotiations of the surrender commenced I began to remember him.

When he entered West Point he was just an average student, but Grant excelled in horsemanship, so much so that he set an equestrian high jump record that lasted for 25 years. And to my surprise, despite his quiet ways he was esteemed by his classmates.

Grant graduated in the middle of his class from West Point and was selected for the infantry. When the Mexican War started he served with distinction under Winfield Scott and Zachary Taylor. It was under Taylor's tutelage that Grant learned his basics of warfare. And it was during the Mexican war that Grant showed his courage and devotion to duty.

As I stated before he was an excellent horseman, calming the animals when others made them balky. But his demeanor was such that he was an introverted man who kept to him self mostly.

Later he got a reputation for drunkenness but I think it was a bit overblown. Perhaps he did drink a bit, but his aide Rawlins told me that when he was stationed far away from his family he missed them terribly. When the Mexican war ended, instead of him being sent home he was stationed to remote outposts in California. That was probably the final straw and the cause of his excess drinking. In my opinion it was here, on the west coast, isolated and away from his family that Grant's habit for drink was formed. And it didn't help that during this trying time he had a martinet of a commanding officer.

It was during one of those depressing times that Grant finally resigned from the army, went back home and tried his hand in business. For seven years Grant toiled at several different jobs but was not very successful.

In 1861 when the War Between the States broke out, and President Lincoln called for volunteers, Grant helped raise a company of soldiers and trained them. But he wanted a command in the regular army, so he contacted Washington, but to no avail.

Soon, Grant started to get noticed in his own state. Wherever he was in command, troop training went smoothly and efficiently. Soon he moved up in grade and eventually President Lincoln himself promoted Grant to Brigadier General.

After victories at Forts Henry and Donelson, Grant was sent, in command, to Shiloh Tennessee.

The two-day battle at Shiloh turned out to be the bloodiest of the war until then.

On the first day of the battle, Grant made a serious blunder. Instead of entrenching his troops, he let them merely bivouac. When the Confederates struck hard they drove the Federal troops back to the Tennessee River where they were saved by the cannons of the Federal gunboats.

Instead of panicking, Grant with his second in command, General Sherman, stayed up late that night studying battle maps.

The next day, reinforced by General Buell, Grant turned the tables and drove the Confederate army off the field, back to the road to Corinth, Mississippi.

The total casualties for the two-day battle for both sides was, 23,000, a figure Washington could not bear, and General Grant was sent into temporary obscurity.

Let me here set down here the reason that General Grant was so valuable to the Federal cause.

A. K. McClure, a friend and confidant to President Lincoln, after Shiloh, went to Lincoln in an agitated state. “First I paced the floor,” he said, “while Lincoln watched me with great interest. Then I stopped and turned to him and shook my right forefinger at him in anger. You must get rid of this drunkard, Grant! He will yet be the ruin of you.”

While I stood there shaking with anger, Lincoln sat very still and silent for a long while, his bearded chin resting on his folded hands. Finally he looked up at me shook his head slightly and said something I shall never forget. "*I can't spare this man Grant; he fights!*"

Then the President smiled and continued. "You see, McClure, if there is a crippling deficiency in the Union army it is a lack of drive on the part of its generals. Oh yes, a few of their men had it, like Kearny, but he was soon killed in a battle.

But on our side there were men like Stonewall Jackson. I never had to give him a second order. When I gave him an order to take a hill, he drove his men with remorseless passion until the job was done.

D. H. Hill was another masterful general. He complained constantly, and told me how wrong I was when we discussed battle plans. But, when I gave him a final order he drove his men with a cold fury that in the end won him great victories.

The other Hill, A. P. Hill was similar, not only in name but in manner. He was incautious, a poor planner and impetuous to a fault. But when ordered to fight he threw everything he had into the fray, defying the odds and providing the murderous drive that invariably won the day.

Then there was my old warhorse Pete Longstreet. He was a fretful and balky man, but when he spotted an opening in the enemy line he struck the enemy's flank like a volcano, no reserve, every man in the assault. He did that very thing at second Bull Run causing a Federal rout.

Until Grant the Federals had no such combative general. Yes, Grant soon had a reputation as a "Butcher" throwing his men wholesale at my army when we were dug in and invulnerable. But as we all know now Grant had a plan and followed it to the end. He kept the other Confederate armies busy with Sherman and Sheridan and finally wore my army down to a frazzle.

Gideon Welles, the Federal Secretary of the Navy had the right idea. He constantly hired and fired men, looking for the one who had that remorseless driving spirit the others lacked. He wanted men who had audacity, an enormous will to succeed during a fierce encounter. And he got it!

Grant, and Sherman and Sheridan had it and that is what beat us in the end."

Our two armies anin't nuthin' but two howlin' mobs

A captured Rebel private

Chapter 30: Into the Wilderness

I began to get reports of Sherman advancing in Georgia, General Sigel with his Federal troops proceeding up our breadbasket, the Shenandoah, and Butler moving up the James toward Richmond. I could now see what Grant's strategy was. He intended to attack Confederate forces on several fronts at the same time so we could not reinforce rebel armies under attack with troops from other areas.

Now it became vital that we defeat Grant here so he would slink back to Washington like all the others did. But that was not to be.

Grant, anxious to get out of the Wilderness, got his army up and on the move by 5 a.m. We were now in a footrace with him over roads that were covered with immovable underbrush, and with vines that grabbed and tripped our feet. In most places, the roads were less than several feet wide.

By 7 a.m. the Federals ran into Ewell's men approaching on the Orange Turnpike. The footrace was over and the battle began!

Union skirmishers were immediately sent out to try and determine whom they were facing and how large the force was. But Meade, thinking it was just a delaying action, wanted to push them aside, and ordered an assault on the blocking force.

Now I became very concerned because Longstreet, who I counted on in this situation, was a full days march away. Thank God we were in the Wilderness. If we were in the open in this situation… I shuddered to think of it.

Grant's plan was to speed through the Wilderness area, go through Chancellorsville, and advance to Spotsylvania Courthouse. Grant was gambling that Meade would get his army past the Wilderness. But Meade suggested the Federals camp for the night and let the supply wagons catch up to the army. A good idea, but Meade forgot one thing, he did not provide proper cavalry coverage to warn of

Confederate presence. This was our chance and we took it.

Grant's army was vastly superior to ours in numbers, but in the Wilderness numbers meant little. The volume of brush and trees allowed for little mobility and visibility. Concealed defenders could decimate blindly charging attackers, and the numerical advantage of the Federal artillery of the attackers was almost useless in the vast snarled forests of the Wilderness. The Wilderness was the great equalizer for Grant's 120,000 men to our 65,000.

My plan was not complex. A.P. Hill and Richard Ewell would move down the Orange Plank Road and Turnpike and stop the Federals in their tracks. Then Longstreet would come in on their flank and crash into the Federals from the thick underbrush around them. Ah, yes, if only Longstreet had been on time.

We then spread the rumor that Stuart was attacking the Federal rear. Mead panicked and sent his cavalry in search of Stuart leaving his main force blind and vulnerable.

By now Longstreet was just 10 miles from the Federal flank, but just as at Gettysburg, Longstreet was tardy. Another opportunity lost by a commander coming in late.

I didn't know it at the time but later, when the two armies camped for the night they were only five miles apart. Before they halted for the night, I brought Hill's men closer to Ewell's divisions for the next day's battle I knew was sure to come. Before I bedded down for the night I instructed Major Taylor to tell General Ewell to resume his march down the Turnpike early the next morning. Should he find the Federal Army at any point he should be cautious, but if possible bring them to battle.

However it wasn't Ewell who precipitated the battle but General Meade who struck first.

As soon as contact was made with Ewell, General Warren was ordered to attack. Thus began the strangest, most heart rending battle of the war. The soldiers fighting the battle were expected to maneuver through overgrown, almost impassable brier patches, pygmy pine trees and vine infested undergrowth.

All over the Wilderness men were ordered to move through smothering thickets to shore up flanks that were up in the air. This became impossible as no one could find their way in this blind maze of jungle. The saving grace was that the enemy could not exploit the danger as they couldn't see the opportunity.

With the situation the way it was, I sent word to Ewell to slow down until Hill could join him. No sooner had I sent the message when Ewell got into the fight of his life. New York Zouves were the opponents and brave to a fault. Again thank goodness for the Wilderness and for the inability to see clearly in the scrub underbrush. That threw the Yankees off to the point where they started to shoot into the backs of their own men. With us shooting at their front and their own men shooting at their backs the Zoaves were staggered.

Both sides, because they could not see clearly to shoot, began bayonet charges. Soon the ground was littered with wounded and dying men while above them the living fought with gun butts, bayonets and fists, each man on his own to fight or die.

Eventually the dry woods caught on fire from the shooting and the flames began to spread. Just like in the battle of Chancellorsville the wounded began to scream as the flames drew near them. They begged their compatriots to help them escape the flames. But like a horrid nightmare, the men fighting above them could not stop the carnage long enough to save their friends.

Ewell's center began to collapse under the Federal numbers and courage. The Iron Brigade had found a hole in the Confederate line and were pouring through. Forgetting his missing leg, Ewell jumped on his horse and raced down the Turnpike to get Jubal Early to shore up his center. Fortunately he met up with John B. Gordon first, and Gordon had fresh troops. They quickly filled up the gap and drove the Iron Brigade back to their starting point. Gordon had saved the day.

Both sides now dug in, their lines only yards apart. Meanwhile little fires kept breaking out and Hill kept moving on the Orange Plank Road. Meade soon began to realize if Hill could take and hold the road junction then Hancock's units would be cut off from the rest of the Federal Army and that would put the entire Federal force in jeopardy. Meade quickly sent a message to Hancock to come to the crossroad with all possible speed. Then he sent for General Getty, another West Pointer. When Getty got to headquarters, Meade explained the situation to him. "Getty, if Hill gets and holds the crossroad our army is split in two and we might as well go home."

Without a moment's hesitation, Getty saluted and said, "General Meade I will hold Hill until the world ends and then I'll fight him in Hell."

Brave words, but hold on he did. Hill had been ill all morning so it was I who stepped in and commanded Hill's troops. We were pushing Getty back but it was no easy task. The Federals held on for dear life and took as many casualties as we did. Finally, at 2 p.m. Hancock showed up. He fell into line with great difficulty as by now the small tangled road was clogged not only with the native forest and underbrush but a myriad of wagons, cannons, troopers and dead and dying men.

Before Hancock could get set, I wanted to order a full assault on his and Getty's troops. My only problem was a two mile gap between Hill and Ewell. If the Yankees could get in there, then we would be split in half. And if anyone could do it, Hancock could.

But Hancock, ignoring the gap, did get set and dug in. Now the two enemies faced each other along a static line and began to feed the Devil his due. The men from both sides lay prone as close to the earth as it was possible to get. Even then both sides exacted a terrible slaughter.

Feeling better, Hill had taken over command of his troops by then, and I sent Veneble to ask if he could hold on. Hill said he could, but asked for me to pray for darkness to come as soon as possible.

Even after dark, soldiers from both sides attacked and countered with muskets and carbines, bayonets and knives. Alas there was no conclusion to these many small fights except to feed the devil with more dead souls.

Finally the firing slowed and eventually stopped. Men from both sides glared at each other through the underbrush while a thick, bluish cloud from the shooting slowly moved up like a billowy blanket then after a while softly and gradually fell toward the ground making visibility even more difficult. Then another sound echoed over the battlefield. Men from both armies were quickly building breastworks and the sound of their axes rang through the forest.

But underneath the sound of axes was a different sound, one full of pain and terror. It was the moans and cries of the wounded from both sides. Men soon forgot their enmities and went out into the no-mans-land to rescue those poor souls who lay in torment. Fires were still springing up and some caught up with wounded men too feeble to escape the flames. It was horrible. I once again thought of what I said at Fredericksburg: "It is well that war is so terrible lest we learn to like it."

The next morning was May 6th and Longstreet was not here yet. Oh how I missed Jackson.

At 5 a.m. Hancock struck. Hill fell back and I ordered Ewell to move to him and help block Hancock. Then I prayed while I looked through my binoculars for Longstreet. But it didn't matter as the Wilderness did what my men could not. Soon after it began, Hancock's assault slowed to a walk as the Federals became disoriented among the undergrowth, vines and trees. Just as a Federal victory looked assured, their charge faltered and became unglued.

At that propitious moment, Longstreet arrived and moved quickly through Hill's tired and spent troops.

In the lead was General Gregg. I rode up to him as shouted, "General, what brigade is this?"

"The Texas Brigade, General."

"Hurrah for the Texas boys. Go and drive out those people." And they did. Forgetting myself I began to ride Traveller to their front to lead them.

"Lee to the rear," they shouted. "Get back, General, get back."

Then Longstreet galloped up and said to me, "General, your line will be secure in an hour if you will permit me to handle my troops. If not I would like to go to some place of safety, as it's not comfortable here."

I laughed at his gentle reproof, assured that our lines would soon be secure.

Longstreet's fresh troops began driving Hancock back. Hancock called for reinforcements to stop the tide but none were available at the time. By 11 a.m. Longstreet had driven Hancock back where he had started. Both sides were now at a standoff.

Longstreet was riding back to me, with his staff, to discuss a new assault when a barrage of rifle fire erupted killing three of Longstreet's staff and wounding the general in the throat and shoulder. He was lifted to the ground and placed in a litter. As they carried him to a surgeon he could hear his men saying, "He is dead!" To counter that thought, Longstreet lifted his hat with his good hand and a cheer went up from his men that could be heard miles away. I soon got word that he would recover. In his absence, I took over his corps. At 4 p.m. I decided to attack. Soon I found that the Federal defense was sound and the attack failed. I then tried a flank charge and did make some headway, but darkness soon put a stop to that.[75] The darkness silenced the guns but not the screams of the wounded and dying. I hear them still, both awake and in my dreams.

---

[75] When Lee attacked the flank panicky officers went to Grant and said, General Lee was cutting them off. Grant got angry and said: I'm tired of hearing what Lee will do. He will not do a somersault and land in our rear and both flanks at the same time. Go back to your command and think of what you're going to do instead of what Lee is going to do.

All day on May 7th I watched and waited for a Federal assault that never came.

Suddenly I realized that Grant was not going to attack, and would not be going back to Washington to lick his wounds either. He was a fighter and fighters don't quit. But where will he go?[76]

Because of his absent cavalry force, we were able to spy on Grant's forces and we discerned his army silently preparing to move.

Now what would I do if I were Grant… Then it came to me like a flash. He is going to maneuver around me and get between me, and Richmond.

"Veneble," I yelled, "get my maps."

After perusing the maps I saw what Grant was thinking. If he could get to Spotsylvania Court House he would have me in a vice.

"Veneble, get the men ready to move."

Veneble handed Lee the maps. "General Lee, does this mean Grant is leaving. If he is, that means you won the battle. Well done, sir."

---

[76] A reporter who was saddling up to go to Washington to file his story, was stopped by Grant. "If you see the President," Grant said, "tell him, from me, that whatever happens, there will be no turning back."

"Won the battle, Veneble? Read me those casualty reports."

"Yessir, I have them right here. The Federals lost 17,666 dead, wounded and missing, while we lost 11,400. You won a decided victory, General Lee."

"You think so Veneble? As good as it seems, this is just what Grant wants. He can afford to lose two men to our one. But it's the one that we lose that is our undoing. You see he can replace his losses, we cannot.

It's now a war of attrition. We either destroy them quickly or die a slow death because of their unlimited numbers and their never-ending supplies.

Richard S. Ewell

Vengeance belongs to God alone

Sir Walter Scott

Chapter 31: Spottsylvania May 8-21, 1864

"Veneble, what time is it?"

"Eight o'clock, sir."

"If Grant were going to attack he would have done it at daybreak – 5:30 at the latest. That means he's not going to attack us, he's going to move…but where…which way…?

That man is a bulldog, Veneble. Now where would he go to bother us the most. Back to the Rapidan?… No, he wouldn't do that… Washington…? No. The other generals might do that after a defeat, but not this man. Let me see that map of this area again."

Damn, I see it now… he's going to Spotsylvania. That would put him astride the road between us and Richmond. Veneble, we must get there before the Federals. Thank God, once more for the Wilderness, he can't move quickly anywhere in here.

Veneble, I want you to go to my engineer division and tell them to corduroy a road directly through the Wilderness from here to the Spotsylvania Court House. And it must be by the shortest route. And it must be NOW!

After you see the engineers, get Major Taylor to go to General Anderson and have him take Longstreet's two divisions on a night march to the Spotsylvania crossroads. When they get there they are to dig in and throw up breastworks. Then, have Generals Hill and Ewell follow Anderson as soon as they are sure the Federals have left their trenches. We must get to Spotsylvania before those people and stop them from getting to Richmond. Do you understand all of that?"

"Yessir."

"Then go, *GO!*"

As I watched Veneble leave the tent I pounded my right fist into my left palm and said aloud, We MUST get there before they do!

As if God, or the fates heard me, a series of events began to occur that allowed us to win this race for survival.

First the Federals got completely bogged down on Brock Road because of too many men, horses and weapons on too small a road.

In addition, because of the milling around of the troops trying to get organized into marching order and blocking the road, Grant and his aides took a shortcut. Unfortunately for them, the shortcut led them right to Longstreet's corps and only quick thinking by one of Grant's aides prevented the Federal commander from becoming a prisoner of war.

Secondly, Anderson's troops were dead tired and needed to rest. But the woods around them were on fire so instead of stopping they kept going. Despite their condition, their continuous marching is what got them to Spotsylvania Crossroads before the Yankees.

And last, but certainly not least, General Sheridan's Federal cavalry had just bested Jeb Stuart at Todd's Tavern and had bivouacked on the side of the road next the Wilderness Tavern. Unfortunately for the Federals, this bivouacking blocked the road and slowed Warren's troops from reaching the crossroads before Anderson.

While Warren was organizing his men to continue their march the sound of carbines firing reached their ears. That was the signal that the thirteen-day Battle of Spotsylvania had begun.[77]

[77] Grant's orders to Meade were to make a forced march during the night of May 7th over two routes to reach the Spotsylvania Court House, 10 miles away. Because of road conditions, burning forests and too many men on a small road, the Federal soldiers could not make a sustained march and the Rebels won the race with little time to spare.

I propose to fight it out on this line if it takes all summer

---

General Grant

Chapter 32: Spotsylvania The Mule Shoe

When Meade reached the Spottsylvania crossroads, he set up his headquarters fully expecting he had beaten me there. He soon found out he was in second place. The Federals immediately attacked, but Anderson's men held off the half-hearted assaults by Warren. By the time Sedgwick joined Warren to strengthen the Federals, Ewell had merged his men with Anderson to make a defensive line that was too strong for the fatigued and exhausted Federals to crack.

The next day the Confederates spent the morning deepening their trenches and building up their earthworks with abatis made of sharpened, felled trees. When they were finished, they glared at their foes, daring them to attack.

By the late afternoon, the Confederate line was formed in a ragged inverted V, with the apex becoming the Mule Shoe, and the sides bent back to meet any flank attack.

Grant then tried to pierce the Confederate line with the now-famous charge by the West Pointer, Colonel Emory Upton.

Upton's idea was to have a compact force four lines deep with three regiments side-by-side in each line. They were to charge the Confederate earthworks, go through and then file left and right and take the Confederates from behind. The second Federal line would then charge and fill in where needed.

Despite the Georgia brigade's desperate stand, the Federals broke through and success seemed assured. But the 12 Federal regiments needed help when they got to the fall back trenches dug by the Confederates.

When I saw the support troops coming, I ordered our artillery to open up on them. The cannons did their work well and the support troops never got more than halfway to our trenches. Now with no support, Upton had to fight his way back. Luckily for him and his men, darkness came and helped them get back to their lines. The charge had cost them 1,000 casualties, but they took back with them 950 Confederate prisoners.[78] I was so upset with the whole affair I never did ask Venable how many casualties we had suffered.

After six days of bloody battle, Grant saw a glimmer of hope in Upton's charge. Then Harrison brought me a Northern newspaper that confirmed Grant's strategy.[79]

What delayed the next assault was not any misgivings about the success of the charge, but the weather. As it had so many times after a battle, the rains came. Not a farmer's rain of gentle drops but a deluge of wind, rain and hail. Before the rain, the men had endured a heat wave, but following the downpour, a cold wind blew over the land that chilled all of us to the bone.

---

[78] Upton's assault gave the Union a distinct gain, but the lack of a spirited dash by the support troops to aid the break-through lost all that might have changed the outcome of the battle.

[79] Grant had sent a note to Halleck stating: We have now ended the sixth day of heavy fighting the result up to this time is much in our favor. I propose to fight it out on this line if it takes all summer

But this change in the weather did not change Grant's strategy. On May 12th, they massed Hancock's troops for the massive assault on the Mule Shoe as soon as light appeared on the horizon.

Before the attack conflicting reports came in from several sources leaving confusion in my mind. To get a better picture of Grant's moves I called a rare conference of my commanders. Generals Ewell, Heth and a very ill A. P. Hill met with me. After much talk, I made my decision. It proved to be erroneous. We would lessen the strength at the Mule Shoe and pull back to be ready to dash in any direction to stay between Grant and Richmond.

As dawn broke the rain continued to soak the ground, lulling my defending troops into a relaxed defensive condition. No one would attack in this weather, they thought. But attack they did. Hancock's 15,000 men charged our line without warning, and once through they moved right and left gathering up like stalks of corn unsuspecting Confederate troopers by the handful.

I had awakened as usual by 3:30 a.m. and was breakfasting when I heard the commotion. The volume of shooting at the

Mule Shoe told me that those people were not retreating but attacking. I dashed to get my horse. Major Taylor had guessed my reaction and had Traveller saddled. I turned the beast and headed toward the shooting. I passed my men running for their lives. "Stop, men! You are deserting your comrades, your cause, your very honor! Stop I say and turn back." I halted Traveller and stared at the men now slowing down. "Shame on you," I said shaking my head, "Your army needs you! Go back, GO BACK!"

But little did I know, General Gordon had already taken charge and was patching together a new defensive line in the middle of the Mule Shoe and directly in front of the oncoming Federals.

I must admit, when I saw the Federals pushing back my boys and crashing through the abatis at the front of the Mule Shoe, I lost my head. I turned Traveller toward the charging Yankees and galloped forward, hatless and weaponless.

It was a good thing General Gordon kept his good sense. He quickly put his horse between me, and certain death. "General Lee," he said calmly, "you cannot lead my men, that's my job. They have never failed you and will not now." He turned to the men. "Will you, boys?"

"No, no!" came the shout. "Lee to the rear, Lee to the rear."

Meanwhile, the Union divisions had turned from a disciplined unit to an unruly mob. They were milling around, leaderless when Gordon's three brigades hit them a hammer blow, staggering the Federals and pushing them back out of the Mule Shoe. But instead of leaving, the Federals turned around and began fighting. Individual clashes broke out in several places along the trenches the Yankees had captured earlier. These Federal men kept their composure, leveled their rifles at the countercharging Confederates and fired volley after volley that stopped the Confederate charge.

Now the fighting turned hand-to-hand, vicious, bloody clashes that asked no quarter and gave none. For hours the fighting continued, the volume of shooting was unparalleled in the worldwide history of warfare. Large trees were felled by errant balls that struck them. Men, too, were decimated by the Minié balls that seemed to be flying everywhere. Men stabbed each other through the logs that bolstered the trenches, while other men sat on the top of those logs and fired down on the unlucky souls in the trenches. It was not long before those on top of the logs firing down on others were soon lying in the trenches, dead.

I had ordered my engineers to build a new defensive line 800 yards from the mule Shoe and told the commanders that the men must hold on until it was completed. I knew they had been fighting and dying since before dawn but they could not yet withdraw. It brought tears to my eyes when I thought of the bodies piled up in the trenches and the falling rain turning red with their blood, but they must stay and fight, and die.

Finally, just a few minutes after midnight the new line was ready. Silently and efficiently the remaining, battered men moved back to the new line. As they moved back, a Union band was playing, Home, Sweet Home. This brought tears to my eyes and I'm sure I was joined by many of the other men.

Dawn, on the 13th of May, brought a macabre sight. The trenches were filled with corpses, and the landscape was a scene from Dante's Inferno. All the trees with a hundred yards of the Mule Shoe were stripped of their leaves, while many of the trees were cut down by the volume of Minié balls. The underbrush was in shreds and many of the dead and mortally wounded lay in every manner of position one could imagine. Once again I thought, *It is well that war is so terrible lest...* Grant spent the next week moving to the left looking for a chance to break our line. Watching him carefully, I countered every move with one of my own.

On May 14th, Veneble brought me the casualty figures. They had lost (killed, wounded and captured) 10,920 men, while we had lost 10,000.[80]

As you can see, Grant's strategy of attrition was working.

And the rains poured down on us unrelenting. It was as if God Himself was trying to cleanse the earth of man's insanity.

From May 12th to May 18th, Grant tried many times to dislodge the Army of Northern

---

[80] Fighting at Spotsylvania occurred on and off from May 8 to May 21, 1864. As Grant tried several tactics to break the Rebel line, in the end, the battle was inconclusive. But with 29,020 casualties on both sides, it was the costliest battle of the campaign. This played into Grant's hands, as Lee had said many times, "It will turn into a battle of attrition."

Virginia to no avail. On May 19th, General Ewell attempted a costly and pointless attack on the Federals and failed to move them.

Tiring of the failures and slaughter, Grant carefully disengaged from the Confederate line on May 21st and moved southeast to once more try and turn my right flank. He could not, and both armies drifted toward the Battle of North Anna.

George Custer

I have always regretted that last assault at Cold Harbor

General Grant

Chapter 33: The Battle of Cold Harbor

At first light on May 27th,General Grant swung wide to the southeast keeping the Pamunkey River between my men and his army. He was doing that hoping to turn my right flank to get between my men and Richmond. It was a waste of time as my cavalry kept their eyes on Grant's movements. And since I had the inside track, for him to get to Cold Harbor, he had to go 40 miles while I only had to go 18.

I had a strong feeling his aim was to go to Cold Harbor because that was the place he could get between me and Richmond.

Little did I know that Sheridan, who could move a lot quicker and easier than Grant's 109,000 man army, would get to Cold Harbor Crossroads before either of us.

As he got there, so did Fitzhugh Lee and his Confederate cavalry. Sheridan got there minutes before Lee, seized the ground and dug in. But Fitzhugh Lee wanted the crossroads and got ready to contest Sheridan for it.

It seemed like a fair fight as the number of men on both sides was about even. The battle was joined and before long it appeared that the Confederates were getting the upper hand.

Before the Confederate cavalry units drove the Federals from the field, here comes another unit pounding across the Pamunkey dashing to Sheridan's side for support. It was Custer and the 1st Michigan. Now there was a difference between the Federals and the Confederates, and the difference was that Custer's men had rapid firing Spencer carbines that could fire 7 or 8 bullets in a minute.

Those carbines made the difference and before long the Confederate horsemen were driven from the field.

Noting that he had lost 256 men as casualties, Sheridan praised the Confederates for their bravery and courage.

No one noticed at the time, but one of the Federal dead was Private John Huff the trooper credited with killing Jeb Stuart.

Now Sheridan and Custer had the crossroads and knowing the Rebels would not let them rest, they began to dig in deeper.

To their credit, the Federal cavalry held the crossroads against several Confederate charges until Grant arrived and had his Infantry take over. Their only problem was that my army showed up at the same time and dug in opposite Grant's troops.

Before long I had my men digging trenches that spanned seven miles at its front.

I must stop here and give the reader a sense of how courageous the men of the Army of Northern Virginia were. By the time they had to dig the trenches, they hadn't eaten for two days. Because of General Breckenridge and his commissary detail, their fast was broken when they were given three biscuits and a slice of bacon. Two days later they got another biscuit. It was very hard to do what my men did on a few biscuits and a slice of bacon.

Hoping to forestall a Grant move around my right, I ordered General Early to strike first. He did against Warren, but he failed to bring up his reserves and Warren handled him easily.

****

Before we got there, Cold Harbor was no more that a quiet, dusty intersection where five roads came together. Its importance came because one road led to Richmond, and another to Federal supplies. Because of Sheridan and Custer, Grant had it, but I wanted it also.

I decided to use Hoke's and Anderson's divisions, with Anderson in charge, to get Cold Harbor back for me. But Grant struck first aiming at the Confederate left.

The Confederates had not been idle. They now had the sharpened stakes of abatis facing the Federals and had finished digging deeper trenches with firing steps, and in some places bombproofs. My plan for the trenches was to stretch them in a crescent for seven miles, anchored on the left by the Totopotomoy River and on the right by the Chickahominy River. Those two bodies of water would prevent flanking moves by the Federals.

Grant wanted an assault before I could get my army completely secure, but his troops were so exhausted by that time, he thought it best to schedule the attack at dawn the next day.

It was a wise move as extremely heavy rain ended all offensive activity for that day.

The 24 hour delay gave the Confederates time to build a secondary trench system with artillery skillfully placed to lay down accurate cross fire against every area of approach. My engineering skills came to the fore and we built a maze of works supported by secondary works. And just like at Fredericksburg, a chicken could not cross any approach at Cold Harbor without being plucked.

At 3:30 a.m. the next morning, the Federals were forming up to attack us. They had no confidence in the charge or their leadership. It was then, I was told, that the Federal soldiers wrote their names and addresses on slips of paper and pinned them on the inside of their jackets so they could be identified and notices sent to their families.

The rain stopped at daybreak and we could see 50,000 of Grant's men coming at us. We were ready.

Holding our fire until the last moment my boys raised up and sent a galling fire into the Federal troops. Their front line tried to run but the men in back stopped them. It was terrible. One of my officers later said to a Federal soldier during a truce to bury the dead, "It seemed like murder to fire so upon you." It was murder, as we fired canister into troops 28 man deep who could not go back or forward. And another Rebel Captain said, "I was at Marye's Heights; but I had seen nothing there to exceed this. This was not war; it was murder."

Because I had the men build the trenches in zigzag fashion they could pour enfilading fire into the lead elements charging at them.

And the trenches these men built were six feet deep with fire steps, behind tangled abatis and chevaux-de-frise. Enclosed forts built on top of the trenches were studded with guns covering large fields of fire. When those people came at us they met up with murderous musket fire, heavy artillery bombs, and marshy ground caused by heavy rains. All together these impediments made the charging troops break up even before they could see the men firing at them. One Federal soldier said he never once saw a Rebel soldier, just the flame and smoke of their guns.

Time after time, the Federals charged until there were 7,000 casualties lying dead or wounded at our front while we had lost a mere 1,500 men.

Foolishly, Meade later ordered another attack. Captain Barker of New Hampshire answered his request by saying, "I will not take my regiment in another such charge if Jesus Christ himself should order it!" His sentiments were echoed by other Federal officers.

For three days the two armies shot at each other without moving from where they were.

When Grant finally realized the magnitude of this defeat he said, "I regret this assault more than any one I ever ordered."

Unable to move forward, Grant then withdrew his army from Cold Harbor and swung wide to the southeast, crossed the

James River to strike at Petersburg, 22 miles from Richmond.

The flanking reads well in the papers but when one has to march day and night it don't go so well

---

Lt. Gerhard Luhn

Chapter 34: JEB Stuart – Yellow Tavern

On May 9th, a hot, steamy morning, 10,000 Federal Cavalrymen, led by the volatile Phillip Sheridan, set out to defeat the indestructible Jeb Stuart and his brave and resourceful band of brothers known as the Confederate Cavalry.

The Federal march to defeat Stuart started with an argument between Sheridan and his commander, General Meade. It went something like this: "General Sheridan, The race to Spotsylvania was lost because your cavalry blocked Warren when he..."

"General Meade," Sheridan interrupted angrily saying, "if you had consulted me BEFORE you deployed my cavalry the night before the race, none of that would have happened.

Dammit, I'm through leading the men. From now on, you take over and give the orders." Storming off Sheridan stopped suddenly and turned around. "And if headquarters would stay out of my business, me and my men would find Stuart and give him the licking of his life."

Now it was Meade's turn to storm off and he went to General Grant to report Sheridan's insubordination.

"Did Sheridan say that?" Grant said in reply to Mead's indignant telling of the conversation. "Well, Sheridan usually knows what he's talking about. Why don't we let him go and do just that?"

****

Reaching Beaver Dam, a forward supply base for the Army of Northern Virginia on their search for Stuart, the 10,000 horsemen led by Sheridan and George Custer set about to destroy my army's supplies. In addition to destroying three weeks of food my army was waiting for, Custer destroyed 25 percent of the Virginia Central's railroad equipment.[81]

By this time Stuart had learned of the location of the Federal cavalry and went after them. Before he left to confront Sheridan, he sent back a report telling me that Sheridan had two ways to go. One was to Richmond and the other to fall on the rear of my army. To counter Sheridan's plan he would split his forces and cover both options. He sent three brigades to me to bolster my rear, and with the rest of his men chased after Sheridan.

To bring Sheridan to battle, Stuart sent Fitzhugh Lee around Sheridan to head him off. Fitzhugh would then attack him from the front while Stuart went at him from the rear.

After giving his subordinates their orders, Stuart did an unusual thing. Thinking he had time he detoured and went to see his wife Flora, and their two children. They were staying at what they thought was a safe haven, at a

---

81 This was an extremely important part of General Grant's overall strategy. Lee's army, and Richmond also, were supplied with their food from the Shenandoah breadbasket by the Virginia Central Railroad.

friend's plantation, a few miles from Beaver Dam. After visiting with his family, he bid them goodbye and reluctantly left them to go back to his troops.

When he got back to his men, the usually jovial Stuart was quiet for a long time. When he finally did speak, it was to his inspector general. What he said upset the inspector so much he wrote it down. When I later read the the paper it said:

I do not wish to live in a defeated South.

When Stuart joined Fitzhugh Lee, he realized Lee was behind Sheridan and not in front as he was supposed to be.

By hard riding, Stuart did get around in front of Sheridan arriving at Yellow Tavern, an old stagecoach stop. There he formed a defensive line and waited for his adversary. A little before noon, Sheridan arrived and the fighting quickly began.

By the middle of the afternoon, both sides had made many charges and counter charges. It was then that Stuart got a message from Richmond telling him that reinforcements were on the way. Heartened he immediately planned a large counterattack on Sheridan's flank. But Sheridan beat him to the punch by attacking first. The lead division of Sheridan's Cavalry had General Custer leading the Michigan cavalry.

To counter the Federal charge, Stuart personally led his final reserve on a decisive countercharge.

Before he charged, his aides pleaded with Stuart to get back, but he laughed and said: "I don't reckon there's much danger. I can't lead from behind no how."

Stuart and the 1st Virginia horsemen soon drove the Michigan men and Custer back. Stuart was in the act of emptying his LeMatt pistol at the retreating Federals when a revolver shot rang out and Stuart slumped in his saddle.

"Are you hit, General?" one of his men asked.

Stuart turned to him and said quietly, "I'm afraid I am."

Stuart start to slide off his frightened mount as his men caught him and lowered him gently to the ground.

After a few minutes, a springless ambulance showed up and Stuart was put on board. The main road to Richmond was blocked by the Federals so Stuart's ambulance had to get to the Capitol by back roads. For six hours the bleeding Stuart had to suffer the agony of a wild journey over rutted roads. He finally reached the home of his brother-in-law Charles Brewer, a physician. By now his wife Flora had gotten word and was on her way to him.

At 7:38 on May 12th, Jeb Stuart breathed his last. As he wished, he would indeed not have to live in a conquered South.

His wife and children reached his bedside just before midnight, too late to say goodbye.

Later that night, I received a telegram. My face turned ashen gray when I opened the telegram and read of Stuart's death. I looked at those around me and said, "Gentlemen I have some bad news. Jeb Stuart is dead." Later, with tears in my eyes, I said, "I can scarcely think of him without weeping."[82]

---

[82] Lee later paid Stuart homage when he told his men, "Stuart never brought me a false piece of information."

The battle of the North Anna River lasted a day or so longer when General Grant was confronted by a wall of Confederate fortifications, designed and supervised by myself.

The defenses were deemed impassable, and by the 25th of May, Grant's men were on the march again. Grant did stop his march for a short while, deciding he would try my right once more. He did not succeed and both armies continued to thrust and parry, with terrific losses in men and materiel on the Federal side. However the losses on our side, though less, were irreplaceable.

Finally, Grant did cross the James River, on June 12th, and his cavalry seized the crossroads at Old Cold Harbor. In several brilliant stands, the Federal Cavalry held the ground and both horsemen again faced each other in a stalemate.

This time there was one big difference in tactics. Because Grant was on the south side of the James River, he would get busy and have his men get after the Southside Railroad, and then finish off the Virginia Central Railroad. Then Grant would be able to cut off all our supply routes except the James River Canal. That which I feared was upon me.

Benjamin Butler

I wish I owned every slave in the South for I would free them all to prevent this war

Robert E. Lee

Chapter 35: The Siege of Petersburg

The battle called the Siege of Petersburg was a complex series of actions over a period of ten months that was spread out over many miles. All this was made even more difficult by the unusual action of blowing up the center of our defensive line by the use of a tunnel. That explosion would evermore be called, *The Crater!*

Grant thought if he went south of the James River, he could capture the Southside Railroad and all the roads leading to Petersburg and Richmond from the major parts of the South.

Also General Hunter, who was destroying southern railroads, would join Sheridan's

Cavalry and together they would come back to Grant. This would add another 18,000 men to the Army of the Potomac. Not enough to equal the amount Grant had lost in frequent battles, but certainly more than I had received.

On June 12th, Grant started moving again. This time there was no Confederate Cavalry to watch his movements and report them to me, so I could then make a blocking move.

The reason I had no cavalry was that I had received a report that Sheridan was going to the Shenandoah Valley and I immediately sent my cavalry to confront him. Sending my cavalry a long way from me was a gamble, but this was a danger I had to risk.

On the 15th of June, Grant succeeded what I feared. He was across the James River, unmolested and on his way to Petersburg and then Richmond. The only thing in his way was fortifications I had designed and some very tough men. The trenches these men occupied were 5 feet deep with tangled abatis and chevaux-de-frise in front. Bombproofs built on top of the trenches were studded with guns covering large fields of fire.

Luckily for the Yankees, these formidable fortifications were not housing my army.

Grant had fooled me with his silent crossing of the James making me move with him.

I did have a scratch force of 1,500 men in the trenches but even the bravest of the brave Confederates would have some difficulty facing 18,000 Yankees.

Of course, we did have Beauregard there, at Bermuda Hundred, but he was facing Butler.

But then fate took a hand again. As they had done so many times before, the Federal Army, through mistaken communications and failure to attack, fouled up a very simple attack plan that would have put them into Petersburg and then into Richmond.

When General Smith, who was the commander of the Federal forces, saw the formidable works in front of him, he reconnoitered until late in the afternoon trying to decide whether to attack or dig in. He finally decided on a third alternative and that was to wait for Hancock to join him in the assault. By the time Hancock arrived and got his men into attack formation, it was 7 p.m.

Of course with only 1,500 men defending, the 18,000 Federals could have easily taken the fort. Now the Federals were in front of their objective with only Beauregard in the way.

About that situation, General Beauregard recently wrote the following to me:

Petersburg at that hour was clearly at the mercy of the Federal commander, General Smith. But instead of continuing on to Petersburg and into the rear of your army, General Smith dallied about until night fell and so did the Federal chances.

Then General Beauregard took a risk only a desperate man would. He emptied the trenches facing Butler and marched the men to Petersburg. In their place, he left a scratch force of pickets and skirmishers to face Butler.

Beauregard's only hope was reinforcements from Richmond and the time to get them. Fortunately for me, he got both.

From June 15th to the 17th, Beauregard held off Smith while he was outnumbered, outgunned and ill supplied. He built three defensive lines and moved into the third one on the morning of June 18th when he welcomed the troops I sent him from the Army of Northern Virginia.

When Hancock saw my troops filing into the defensive line he went over and had words with General Smith. When he was finished, he angrily left and reported to General Grant. When Grant heard about the missed opportunity, he shrugged his shoulders and went back to plans for severing the Southside Railroad line.

Although Smith had made some error, it was the Federal staff work of the Army of the Potomac that was really at fault. The staff got the Federals out of Cold Harbor brilliantly, but this day, fate was on our side.

Pierre Beauregard

Peace cannot be held by force...only by understanding

Albert Einstein

Chapter 36: Beauregard Saves the Day

Somehow, whether it was because it was always there, or because Grant was now facing me at critical times, the Potomac Army always seemed a little out of control. When an order was given, the execution of that order was misunderstood or ignored. Even with Grant in charge, when an order was given, between the order and the result there always seemed to be a flaw. Thus it was when the Federal army was on the doorstep to Petersburg, and the end of the war could be seen.

Butler got his reinforcements, but was at a loss about what to do with them. When I saw the situation I took immediate action and sent reinforcements to Beauregard and once more that movement of my men sealed Butler's fate and put him completely out of the war, this time for good.

On the other front Meade had ordered the Army of the Potomac to assault Beauregard at dawn. If they had done so, they could have walked over Beauregard and waltzed into Petersburg. But somehow all the Federal generals seemed to be in a daze that morning and not one of them, even Hancock, could generate enough pluck to push through Beauregard and take the ripe plumb of Petersburg.

When Hancock reported to Meade, and Meade came to the front and saw what was happening, he erupted with a string of oaths that could be heard a mile away. Meade learned that Lee's troops had not yet reached Beauregard and ordered an attack all along the line. When nothing happened, Meade ranted and railed and still got no result. After a while, a fuming Meade watched as the hard driving Rebels arrived and filled in the line next to Beauregard's tired but happy troops.

Beside himself with rage at his generals' incompetence, Meade stormed about and then told the generals to charge when they were ready. They eventually did attack but it was disorganized, ineffective and expensive in Federal lives.

In the past four days, the Federals had lost another 10,000 men due to the unbelievable incompetence of their leadership.

Now the war of flanking and maneuvering and hard marching was over. For the next ten months both armies would fight a trench war, twenty-five miles long. This would be a stationary war of snipers and shelling and deprivation that would try the sanity of men on both sides.

****

Both armies now dug in so deeply they could not be moved. Each side brought up Coehorn mortars that could lob shells at the other's trenches making lives miserable and dangerous. And should a man raise his head above the trench opening a sniper would immediately get a bead on him and take him out. For the ten months, Union and Rebel alike faced each other like rats living in a maze.

As I had said many times before, if Grant can't be stopped and gets us in a siege at Richmond, it would then just be a question of time before we were finished. Well I was not exactly at Richmond, but very close to it.

At least there was one ray of hope. Since General Breckenridge was now in charge of supplies, my army was no longer starving. And we even had new uniforms to give them, and weapons and ammunition to fight with. Bless that man, Breckenridge.[83]

The war with Grant now came down to a series of thrusts by him, and a parry for each of the thrusts. Most of the attacks Grant made were aimed at the railroads and waterways that supplied my troops. My blocking action was successful in holding Grant for ten months.

But Grant had other problems. Although my army was a good deal smaller than his, we had killed or wounded about 64,000 of his men during his Overland Campaign. In addition, many of his troops had their enlistments ending and they were leaving the Union army in a steady stream.

---

[83] It didn't last. Breckenridge tried but the supplies just weren't available.

As I have said many times, Grant could make up his losses and I could not. And he certainly did. Grant and his provosts did the job, with reenlistments by men who wanted to stay to the end. Combing through the troops in the rear and bringing in the troops in Washington that weren't needed there, they refilled their ranks. Soon, those men were facing us at the front. And us? Well, they don't come any braver than those men who held off the Federal Army at Petersburg, but they were not going to be reinforced.

George Meade

The siege is working, let it be

The Crater was the saddest affair I have witnessed in this war

General Ulysses Grant

Chapter 37: The Crater

Heeding the cry from the people up north who were tired of the war, General Grant brought Meade into the headquarters tent for a conference. Proposing some kind of assault to break my line was on Grant's mind and he spoke to his subordinate about it.

After Grant laid his plan out, Meade's reply was clearly stated: "Lee is too strong and now that he is decently supplied with weapons he is even stronger than before."

"Yes," Grant replied, "but many of his men are crossing over to us every day."

"Yes they are, but it's because they are hungry and their families are starving, too. The eight dollars we are paying for their rifles when they surrender will save their families from starvation. The siege is working, let it be."

"You know, Meade, at Vicksburg the siege worked fine. The city was surrounded, cut off completely from food and ammunition. But here, at Petersburg, they are not surrounded.

The railroads are still running, and I am getting a lot of pressure to end this stalemate."

"What I'm thinking is something like Upton did at the Mule Shoe at Cold Harbor. Not a quick affair, but one where we scouted the ground we have to traverse, and pick the right leaders to lead the charge."

Meade shook his head, but Grant ignored that and kept on speaking.

"Let me tell you what Burnside has come up with. His men have been digging a mine shaft."

"A mine shaft?"

"Yes, a mine shaft. Part of Burnsides men, the 48th Pennsylvania, are from coal country. One of their pickets, a private, was looking over at the Rebel line and mused, "Why don't we dig a shaft under them, plant a few kegs of gunpowder under them and blast the whole bunch of Rebs to their Maker."

"The private went to his colonel with the idea and was sent up the line to Burnside. Word got to me and the more I thought about it, the more I liked it. It fit right into my plan to assault their center."

"But I got word from Washington that things were jittery there because Jubal Early came to call and I had to send part of my army to cut him off. Now the mine loomed even more important to the attack plan. Less soldiers to assault and more gunpowder for the blast."

Meade agreed and the fiendish plan was set for July 30th at dawn.

Somehow the boys on our line knew about the shaft and even made jokes about it. Had I been informed about the digging, I would have at least made a second line of defense for the men attacked to fall back to.

Burnside had four divisions. One division was made up of colored troops who volunteered to make the charge after the gunpowder went off. Meade turned them down as he thought it would look like he was sacrificing the black troops in a charge that was bound to fail.

The honor then went to Burnsides First Division led by General Ledlie. It could not have been a worse choice.

Men under Ledlie said he was a drunkard and a coward. On the morning of the Crater, both turned out to be true.

Basic preparations for the blast and charge were ignored except for the part played by the miners.

On July 30th, the shaft was finished, the First Division was set, the fuse was lit, and promptly went out.

A miner was sent in to find out what was wrong. All the way to the splice that had come apart, he thought only of his mortality. When he found the separation he, re-tied it, lit it again and crawled, and then ran for his life.

At five o'clock on July 30th, the gunpowder went off like an earth shattering volcano blowing the Rebels manning that part of the line, to eternity.

To the men watching, both Yankee and Rebel, the shower of rock, dirt, timbers and parts of men were unbelievable, more like a hellish part of a nightmare than a dream.

The Federal troops were then to charge through the gap turn right and left in back of the Confederate line and take them out while the second unit of Federals charged the front.

But, true to their fumbling hearts, when the Federals got to the crater instead of going around they stopped and gaped at the large hole that had formed. No one had told them to go around the crater so they marched right into that man made depression. Now there were hundreds of them sliding down on the sides and milling about the bottom. It took the good part of an hour for the Rebels to recover from the shock of the explosion and start firing shells into the crater. Also my very angry veterans got on the rim of the crater and began shooting into a helpless, milling mass of Federal soldiers. On top of that, some officer ordered the colored troops to follow the whites to the crater. That just infuriated the Rebels even more and now the entire crater became a killing field.

Where was the commanding officer[84] to guide those errant troops? He was hiding in a bombproof like a coward, and drinking himself

[84] General Grant found out later that not only was Ledlie hiding in a bombproof, but none of the other division commanders in this corps were up front to guide their men.

into a stupor like a drunkard. Ledlie's critics were right.

The total of Federals killed at the crater was almost 6,000 men. Not a lot by all the recent battle casualties, but enough for the Committee on the conduct of the war to call for a court of inquiry.

I think Grant summed it up well when he spoke at the inquiry: "...I believe the cause of the disaster was the leaving of the passage of orders from one to another down to an inefficient man..."

Hell is empty...all the devils are here

William Shakespeare

Chapter 38: Fort Steadman

General John Gordon entered my headquarters tent and doffed his hat while I was bent over my map table looking for a spot to charge through Grant's line.

He saluted and said, "You sent for me, General?"

I returned his salute and bade him to come over to the map table. "Yes, General Gordon, I need your advice. As you assuredly know we are facing calamity. Our boys are cold, tired and hungry. Grant is gradually moving left stretching our line so thin it will soon break. I don't know if the boys could withstand another assault by Grant. The reason I called you here is because you being on the line, know best what we are facing, and you're more sensible than most of my generals.

What I am proposing may be a last-gasp offensive. What I am looking for is a weakness in Grant's line that I can smash through and clean out a portion of the Federal line. Then I can threaten his supply depot at City Point. If we're successful and having a shorter line to defend I could send half my army to Johnston in South Carolina. He can then defeat Sherman and come back and join us to face Grant together."[85]

I paused and let my words sink in. "Of course, with just a half of an army here we would be vulnerable to Grant. What I really would like to do is to break through and march my *whole* army to South Carolina, feed them, and then join up with Johnston." I waited quietly for an answer from Gordon.

He stood quiet for a full minute and then spoke softly. "General, these boys of mine will go anywhere and do anything for you. But in their present condition do you think they are

---

[85] This was pure wishful thinking. Grant would not react to a small breakthrough with all the thousands he had on the Federal line.

capable of breaking through this Federal line of well-fed, well-clothed troops, and then march hundreds of miles to General Johnston?"

Now I was thoughtful. "No, but I would give them extra rations, have them spend a half day in Richmond and let them rest. Then I would bring them back and ask them to do the impossible. You see, Gordon, we are on our last legs. If we don't do something, we may have to surrender.

Gordon stiffened at the word "surrender".

"Then General, we have no choice. In my opinion the best place to break through the Federal army is here!" He pointed, at Fort Steadman.

"I totally agree with you, General Gordon."

He saluted and said, "Let me get my men ready and I'll be back with a plan of attack."

"Good. I will send over the extra rations."

Gordon turned to leave.

"General Gordon, I know it's a gamble but to stand still in this situation is nothing but death."

Without another word Gordon left. My aide, Major Taylor was working at his desk and had heard every word. When Gordon left he got up and said, "General Lee, I would like to be in the charge with General Gordon, Sir."

I smiled at him. "I wish I could spare you, Major Taylor, but I need you here."

****

As I had done before at Chancellorsville, I split my forces in half giving Gordon one half, four and a half divisions, and leaving the other half on the line facing Grant.

On March 25th at 4 a.m., the men were ready. They were to be led by North Carolinians who held axes instead of rifles. At the start signal, the axmen were to charge in and chop through the sharpened cheveaux-de-frise. They were to be followed rapidly by two regiments at quickstep.

The Federal pickets were so used to large groups of Rebels coming through and surrendering they let my men pass without questioning. After a few moments the pickets realized what was going on and they had time for one rifle shot. They killed and wounded quite a few of our boys with that shot but we overwhelmed them quickly.

The gunfire alerted the Yankees in Fort Steadman and they sent a galling fire into our troops. However in a short time we prevailed and captured the fort and many of the soldiers within. The remaining men of Fort Steadman kept their cool and retreated while firing at the invaders.

Although it was a confusing fight in the dark, both sides managed to stay steady. Our artillerists turned Fort Steadman's guns on the Yankees and enfiladed the entrenchments to the right and left. Meanwhile, the Federals formed a defensive line and made a stand.

Now the attackers faced a serious problem. In front of them they faced a series of earthworks and trenches. In daylight they could easily traverse them, but in the dark it was a different story.

Both sides were now firing artillery, with effect, into the other's troops. "The air was so full of shells," one soldier said, "It resembled a flock of birds with fire in their tails."

Inside Fort Steadman both sides came together too close to fire at each other and began close order battle using their rifles as clubs and their fists as in a drunken brawl.

When Gordon reached Fort Steadman he sent a note to me saying everything was well in hand, but that was not the case. The cavalry that was supposed to follow the troops in for mop-up were lost in the maze of trenches. And many of our boys could not resist the rations they saw lying around the fort, and stopped to consume them.

By now Grant's entire army was coming awake and began to act resolutely. They moved in and virtually surrounded the Confederates, who, like the Union soldiers at the crater, were now milling about.

When he saw the Federal troops all around his men, Gordon acted decisively. He sent a message to me telling of the men's bravery, but that they could not overcome the massive Federal presence. Reluctantly I ordered the men back to our lines. The attack of Fort Steadman had failed and we lost some 2,000 men. This set up the defeat at Five Forks and the loss of Petersburg on April 2nd and 3rd. Now I knew our cause was lost. *It's only a matter of time.*

That man Grant will fight us every hour and every day until the end of the war

---

General James Longstreet

Chapter 39: Five Forks (The Great Shad Bake)

On March 28, 1865 Grant, Sherman, Porter and President Lincoln met in the cabin of the River Queen. They had a long and profitable social visit.

The next day the three men again met with the President, this time to discuss the strategy they planned to use against me and General Johnston. Lincoln expressed the hope that the battles would soon be over and that the Rebels would surrender peaceably.

Then the subject of guidelines for the surrender came up.

Lincoln answered succinctly and summed up his strategy for when the South surrendered.

"Let them once surrender and go home and swear not to take up arms again. Let them go, officers and all... I want no more bloodshed."[86]

After the meeting the generals and the President returned to their respective jobs.

When Grant got back to his men, the final act of stalemate at Petersburg came to an end with lightning speed.

****

On Sunday March 26th, an important courier slipped into St. Paul's Episcopal Church he knew President Davis frequented. Trying to be as innocuous as possible, the corporal moved silently down the pews toward the president.

The preacher, Mr. Minnegerode, was speaking in loud resonant tones when he spied the corporal. His speech then slowed down, and stopped altogether when the courier handed the president a paper. Everyone in the church, by then had his eyes riveted on the

---

[86] This was a far cry from the reality after Lincoln's death. Stanton and the new president, Andrew Johnson had vengeance on their mind. They jailed Davis and talked about hanging Lee.

President. No one spoke and it was as if the silence was actually painful.

As he read the message, President Davis' face turned ashen gray. After he finished reading, he crushed the message in his fist and stared into space. He sat motionless for a full minute then shakily got to his feet. Five or six men scattered around the church rose up when he did and all of those men surrounded the president and ushered him out of the church.

While Davis was leaving, he dropped the message. A man sitting at the edge of the pew nearest the paper reached out and picked it up. He stood up and held it out toward Davis, but the president had already left. Sitting back down the man opened the crushed message and began to read aloud:

Mr. President:
I advise that all preparations be made for leaving Richmond tonight. It is my sad duty to report to you that Petersburg and Richmond are doomed. I now must move my army in the face of the enemy, meet up with

Johnston, and continue the fight elsewhere.

It is my opinion that you must move the government somewhere else as I can no longer protect Richmond from General Grant.

Your Obedient Servant,

R.E.Lee

****

For more than a month, General Grant had suspected that I might move out of Petersburg and affect a melding of my troops with General Johnston's. Somehow I knew that when that day came he would try to block any movement I made. I was right, and soon he began to move his men into a blocking position. But in moving, he began to see a chance to force me out of the trenches at Petersburg. To obtain that end, he sent Warren's troops around my right to outflank me, forcing my men to leave the safety of their trenches.

On the morning of March 29th I began to see what Grant was doing and I reacted. I pulled Pickett's division out and joined him with Thomas Rosser and my son Rooney. Then I put Fitzhugh Lee in charge of all of them. Fitzhugh Lee now had a force of 5,500 men. Not nearly what the Federals had, but we had no choice, we had to make the move.

Grant saw the possibilities of flanking us at Five Forks and sent his men driving forward in the rain to get there first. Luckily for us, Fitzhugh Lee had arrived at Five Forks just before the Federals got there. Not having time to entrench the two armies immediately got into heavy skirmishing. But by then the heavy rain began to turn the ground into mud.

Grant arrived at the battlefield and watched his men sliding around in the mud trying to drag an artillery piece to a place where they could fire on the Confederates. Soon the piece, the men and the horses were knee deep in the mud and stuck there.

By noon, Grant had had enough and called the men back. He told Sheridan, "It's impossible for us to do much until it stops raining and dries up a little."

That evening, a dismayed Sheridan rode the seven miles to Grant's tent. He dismounted, slapped his hat on his knee to rid it of the rain and went inside. Not stopping to greet Grant he immediately began pacing. In a few moments he stopped and turned to Grant. “General, I’m ready to strike out tomorrow and go to smashing things...” Sheridan continued to press his case and soon Grant held up his hand to stop the tirade.

He reached into his jacket pocket and took out two cigars. He lit one and offered the other to his cavalry chief. After a few puffs Grant looked up at the expectant Sheridan, gave him a beatific smiled and said, “Sheridan, let’s do it! Get your men ready and we’ll go in tomorrow and smash things!”

****

Well, the Confederacy might have been on its knees, but I wasn’t. The next morning the rain stopped and Sheridan showed up at Five Forks to “smash things.” There he found Pickett with cavalry.

Sheridan had Gouverneur Kemble Warren for support, but Sheridan did not trust him. Although Warren had been a hero at Gettysburg, as the war went on he became abrasive and exceedingly moody. Sheridan had asked Grant to get someone else, but in the hectic time of getting ready for the battle of Five Forks, nothing was done.

The next day, thinking this would be a lark against Pickett, Sheridan ordered a charge large enough to push Pickett out of his breastworks. I had also sent Fitzhugh Lee to Five Forks with infantry to back Pickett up. He arrived just in time to join Pickett's troops as Sheridan was about to assault him.

Now it was Sheridan's turn to worry. Instead of attacking, Sheridan found he was in the embarrassing position of having to defend his cavalry and himself against Pickett's infantry.

For the rest of the day, there were charges and counter charges by both sides until finally the setting sun and the following darkness stopped the fighting.

Warren was also having trouble with Bushrod Johnson's Rebels and before nightfall, only a furious charge led by Joshua Chamberlain saved the day for Warren's Federals.

The next day the rain stopped and Sheridan waited impatiently for the field to dry. When the field was halfway dry he started his attack.

But this was Pickett's day and when Sheridan charged, Pickett's Confederate cavalry hit the Federal flank and drove Sheridan's men back. Sheridan then called in Custer and Devin. With this new support Sheridan, with Custer at his side, barely withstood Pickett's well-conceived and executed plan. Only the darkness saved the Federals from utter defeat.

Now Sheridan's sharp military eyes spotted a flaw in Pickett's dispositions. To do what they did to him, the Confederates had to get out of their trenches. And away from their trenches, they were vulnerable.

As Sheridan then said, "We have at last drawn Pickett's army out of its fortifications. This is our chance to finish them."

General Warren also realized Pickett was vulnerable. He suggested to Grant that he attack one side of Pickett while Sheridan catches them in a pincer as he assaults the other side.

Grant approved Warren's plan and told Sheridan that Warren would be ready to attack by midnight.

As usual there was a glitch in the Federal plan and Warren was not in position until 6 a.m. the next morning.

At daybreak Pickett saw how exposed he was. Although Sheridan had also been pushed back severely, Pickett was also in some difficulty. He quickly moved his men from his exposed position to one of less danger.

Sheridan wanted to attack right away, but Warren was still not quite ready.

When I observed this last move of Pickett's, I got angry and send him this curt order:

I regret exceedingly your forced withdrawal, and your inability to hold the advantage you had gained. Now you must go back to Five Forks and stay there. You must now hold Five Forks at all hazards!

After Pickett read the order he reluctantly went back to his old breastworks at Five Forks and set his men up for defense.

Pickett waited all day for a Federal attack but none came.

Then he got a second message but this time it was a pleasant one from his subordinate, General Tom Rosser. It was a note for both Pickett and Fitzhugh Lee, inviting them for a shad fish dinner, caught fresh by Rosser in the nearby Nottaway River.

The Federal infantry had not come back all day, and if the Yankee cavalry attacked without infantry, the Confederates felt certain they could fight them off.

Besides, the generals were both hungry, and the shad, baked or fried, would hit the spot.

Pickett and Fitzhugh Lee felt confident they could take some leisure time with Rosser and go to the shad bake. Since they were regular army, the fact that they never told anyone that they were leaving, and worse yet, did not leave anyone in charge, I found worthy of a court martial.

What they both told me later was that they were sure if trouble came they would hear the firing and come back quickly. The trouble was they never heard anything.[87]

---

[87] Porter Alexander, the Head of artillery for the Army of Northern Virginia

Rosser was an excellent host and cook. By the time the three generals finished their food and drink it was 4:15 p.m.

Meanwhile Pickett's non-coms could see Sheridan's Federals massing for an attack. Fifteen couriers were sent in a dozen directions to find the generals. Eventually every one of the couriers came back empty handed.

Then the battle began. As had happened so many times before the Federals botched the beginning drive, and when the Confederates leveled their first volley at them it staggered the Yankee line and left them in disarray.

Luckily for them they had a cool head with them, and very soon General Chamberlain straightened them out. After that, Sheridan took over and with inspired leadership, led his troops onward.

Meanwhile Pickett, still unaware of the ferocious battle occurring just a little over a mile away, was lying back in the grass enjoying the glow of a satisfying meal and a

---

said, upon hearing Pickett say he did not hear the gunfire commented: "It was perhaps owing to a peculiar phenomenon of acoustic shadows."

drink or two. Suddenly he felt a slight nagging fear in his stomach. *I've been away from the troops for quite a while. Maybe I should send a message back and make sure everything is okay.*

Pickett sat up and called two of his runners over. He wrote out two notes and handed them to the couriers. "Come back as soon as you can boys, and let me know how things are." Then Pickett, chewing on a piece of straw, lay back down again.

As soon as the couriers crossed Hatcher's Run, Pickett heard a burst of firing. He sat up quickly just in time to see one of the couriers being captured by several Federal soldiers.

Jumping up and racing to his horse, Old Black, Pickett quickly mounted and started to gallop, as fast as the horse would go, back toward Five Forks. In a few minutes, he saw blue uniforms and quickly realized that he was cut off from his command by a company of Federals at his front. He turned his horse around and looking for a way around the Federals, fortunately ran into some Confederate cavalry scouts. Pickett quickly explained the situation to the cavalry commander.

The Confederate cavalry then lined up and led a charge for him, and freed him to get back to his men.

But he got there too late. Although Pickett and his men gave a valiant account of themselves trying to get their previous positions back, they had been leaderless too long. The Federals were too full of elan to let them take their defensive trenches back.

By 6:45 that evening, the last Confederate resistance collapsed, and more than 5,000 Rebel soldiers were captured.[88]

A Confederate Captain wrote in his diary after the battle: *It has been an evil day for us. My heart sickens as I contemplate recording this day's disasters.*

[88]5,000 Confederate soldiers had been captured at Five Forks. After the battle, the Federal Provost Marshall herded the men into a field and addressed them. He told them that anyone who signed the Oath of Allegiance to the United States could go home right away. 100 soldiers signed to the derision and then shunning of their fellow prisoners.

A few more Saylor's creeks and it will be all over

General Robert E. Lee

Chapter 40: Saylor's Creek

Now the race to join General Johnston began in earnest. Lee and his entire army started north toward Carolina.

I must galvanize my men to get ahead of the Yankees, get some food in their stomachs and march like furies to get to General Johnston. Then we will turn on the Yankees and together whip them.

The only problem was that Grant was the other horse in the race and though he had a slower horse, it was well fed and had plenty of ammunition. And the jockey on that Federal horse was named Sheridan, and he was relentless.

I had ordered my commissary people to have rations for the men at Amelia Court House. When we got there, I moved rapidly to the rail cars and the promised food. I was so excited to have my army fed that I opened the nearest boxcar and peered inside. Where there should be rations there was none. I was mortified when what I found was naught but harnesses and ordnance.

When I got over the shock of no food for my men, I found a blocking force of Federals on the road to Danville.

I immediately changed orders and re-directed the men to our supply depot at Farmville. Hungry and exhausted, we marched all night on April 5th.

On April 6th the rain came and slowed us even more. We couldn't slow much more as we were being pursued by the Union Second Corps. To make matters worse Sheridan's cavalry rode parallel to us striking us with hit-and-run raids like angry wasps. To my dismay, there was also Yankee Cavalry blocking the road to Farmville.

With Sheridan on one side and a blocking force in front, we were in a vise. Now we had to stop, organize an assault and fight our way out. This became the Battle of Saylor's Creek.

Ewell's men deployed near Little Saylor's creek and dug in while Wright's Federal Corps formed opposite him. The Federals had artillery and unfortunately, General Ewell had none. After shelling Ewell's men for 30 minutes, the Yankees waded across the creek and charged the Confederates. Ewell's men stood up and let loose a volley that staggered the first line of the Federals, and the rest of them dropped down for cover.

Seeing the Yankees stopped, another Confederate brigade on Ewell's right charged the Yankees. But it was too little and too late.

By now a great many more Federals crossed the creek and slammed into the charging Confederates. That brigade was no match for the Federal numbers and they either surrendered or died.

The Federals didn't stop there. After dealing with the brigade they kept moving until they hit Ewell's flank causing many of his sleepless and exhausted men to also give up their guns in surrender.

Down the line the Confederates fared no better. General Custer assaulted Pickett's division while Merrit's cavalry pressed both flanks. Custer finally broke through and those men that didn't surrender, skedaddled for the rear. Seeing all this surrendering and running I could not help but say out loud, "My God, is my army dissolving?"

Sheridan, watching all of this, went to Grant and said, "If the thing is pressed I think Lee will surrender."

Grant nodded his head and said, "Let the thing be pressed."[89]

---

[89] April 6th 1865 became known to the Confederates as "Black Thursday." In the three battles along Saylor's Creek, Lee lost almost a fourth of his army, and the Federals revealed that they captured six generals, including Lee's son Custis, General Ewell and 7,000 enlisted men.

We came to Mclean's house very much as people enter a sick-chamber expecting to find the patient very ill

General Horace Porter

Chapter 41: The End of the Road[90]

A Confederate General on General Beauregard's staff once said to him, "Beast Butler was the one Yankee that if captured, would be shot without trial. It turned out that General Grant thought of him much the same way.

When General Beauregard pulled his troops out of Bermuda Hundred to save Petersburg, Benjamin Butler and his army did

[90] I am sometimes criticized for letting the war go on for so long. But I did only what my duty demanded. I could have taken no other course without dishonor and if it all would be done over again I would act in precisely the same manner. General Robert E. Lee.

nothing. Petersburg was totally unprotected and yet Butler would not move. His subordinate commanders, along with Grant, saw the opportunity, but Butler's non-military mind could not comprehend the prospect of striking my rear.

Responding to Grant's command to get going, he did give orders but they were confusing, and late. The Federal soldiers were disordered by the chaotic commands and by the time his responsible front line commanders straightened everything out, I had sent Pickett in to block the Federal assault, push it back, and once more seal up Bermuda One Hundred, this time for good.

"Beast" Butler was a shady fellow. A good example of his slippery behavior was in 1860 when he said he would not interfere with slavery in a slave state. But when he was the authority in New Orleans after the war started, it was suggested to him to put Southern Negroes in the Federal army. He said, "Absolutely not."

Corruption hung about him like a clinging, gaseous fog. Some of it was rumor, but most of it turned out to be true. When he was military governor in Louisiana, he hung a man illegally[91]. When the women of New Orleans would cross the street to avoid a passing soldier, and would completely ignore Federal soldiers when they were spoken to, he became infuriated.

The final insult was when the women spit on the Federal uniforms when his men approached, he then figured a way to insult the women of New Orleans by threatening them with being treated as "ladies of the night" if they disrespected his soldiers in any way.

The infamous proclamation to stop this degradation of Federal soldiers was issued as "Order #2" as follows:

---

[91] Butler hung a man named Mumford for tearing down a Federal flag

> As the officers and soldiers of the United States have been subjected to repeated insults from the women (calling themselves ladies) of New Orleans, in return for the most scrupulous noninterference and courtesy on our part, it is ordered that hereafter when any female shall, by word, gesture, or movement, insult or show contempt for any officer or soldier of the United States, she shall be regarded and held liable to be treated as a woman of the town plying her avocation.

Scandal, involving Butler, was always just around the corner but never quite proved.

Grant was absolutely disgusted with the man and his lack of Military ability. Men were dying because of Butler's ineptness and Grant swore to get rid of him. But getting rid of this blight on the Army of the Potomac would prove to be more difficult than cornering my Rebel Army. You see, Grant did corner us but he never did nail Butler.[92] That unworthy gentleman had an ace in the hole that Grant was completely ignorant of. Since 1864 was a Presidential election year, and Butler was the darling of the abolitionists, he led a large part of the voters, and had influence with certain members of the electorate who could bring about the loss of the presidency for Lincoln.

General Grant was a practical man, a middle of the country boy, one to whom a man's word was his bond. Now he had a general who was a little on the slick side and he didn't like it.

To Grant there was a simple solution, fire the man! Even General Halleck, the Chief-of-Staff understood Grant's problem. He had written a letter some time ago to Grant's friend, General Sherman, that said: "It seems little better than murder to give important commands to such men as Banks, Butler, McClernand, Sigel and Lew Wallace, yet it seems impossible not to because of their influence on Congress and the voters."

---

92 Grant did have him kicked upstairs by having Halleck appoint him to an administrative position away from military commands.

So it was that opportunity was lost for the Federals. But as I have said several times before, it seem ordained that the Federal army would almost get to success and then once more slip and fall.

****

It was April 4th and hunger rode along with us and took more of my men out than Federal bullets did.

Sheridan wanted to get in front of us and captured documents told us he had asked Meade's permission to do that. Meade said, "No", but that didn't stop Sheridan and he went over Meade's head to Grant. A while later, Meade was surprised at a visit from Grant. The general told Meade what Sheridan had said, but Meade was adamant and said he would not move until dawn the next day. When he did move, to his discredit, it was in the wrong direction.

I knew the Federal Cavalry was at Jetersville and that they could be easily brushed aside. But when we got there, we found that along with the cavalry there was also Federal infantry.

I then swung my army around and headed toward Lynchburg where there was food for my army and a solid road to Johnston's army.

We marched all that day and then through a night of heavy rain.

By now my worn out, exhausted and starving soldiers had no idea where they were or how they got there. Many wandered away searching for food while others just fell on the road and slept or just lay there in a stupor.

I heard later that one of my stragglers was sitting by the side of a stream when a Federal soldier came upon him and pointed his rifle at him. The Yankee said, "I gotcha." "Yeah," the ragged and starving Southern boy replied, "you got me, an' a hell of a git you got."

Meanwhile the poor Southerners not only had to keep going, but they had to fight off Sheridan's cavalry as periodically they would pounce on the Rebel line in a hit and run fashion.

When dawn broke on the 6th, I realized we were just a few miles from Rice's Station and food. But as we struggled toward our goal Gordon had to continually fight of Federal attacks at the rear of our line. One could only marvel at the courage displayed by our defenders despite their exhaustion and hunger.

Several severe battles took place now including a battle for the Appomattox Bridge that we had to have if we were to get to Johnston. Thank God the Appomattox Bridge battle was a complete victory for us. In addition, we took over 800 Federal men prisoners there.

My plan never changed. I was going to Farmville, feed my men and then go over the Appomattox Bridge to join Johnston. Now that we were really close, I let myself think that once we got over the Appomattox Bridge, we would set fire to it and get some breathing room.

We again marched through the night, staggering on without strength for anything but putting one foot in front of the other and moving forward. By early morning we were filing through the streets of Farmville, and by God's grace, each man was holding his ration of corn and bacon. My army was saved, or so I thought.

Little did I know that instead of destroying the bridges after they crossed some of my troops got into a furious fight and the bridges were saved by some bravery on the part of the Federal soldiers.

That night Grant got word from Sheridan. Lee's supplies are 26 miles away at Appomattox Station. If I can beat Lee to the supplies, the chase might be over.

With that heartening news Grant sat down and began to write a message to me:

The result of the last week must convince you of the hopelessness of further resistance on the part of the Army of Northern Virginia, I feel that it is so and regard it as my duty to shift from myself the responsibility of any further effusion of blood, by asking of you the surrender of that portion of the Confederate States army known as the Army of Northern Virginia.

When I got the message later that night, I showed it to Longstreet who was at my tent. His reply was succinct, "Not yet."

Since none of my aides was in the tent I sat down and wrote in my own hand a reply.

Though not entertaining the opinion you express of the hopelessness of further resistance on the part of the Army of Northern Virginia, I reciprocate your desire to avoid useless effusion of blood, and therefore, before considering your proposition, ask what terms you will offer on condition of its surrender.

After writing the note I sent orders out for a march to Appomattox Station where supplies from Lynchburg lay unguarded nearby. First we had to quickly disengage from the Federals and get to Appomattox Court House for the supplies.

On a spring morning, April, 8th, we began to quietly disengage from the Federals and march toward our goal. Before we went a mile a courier came racing along with an answer from General Grant. I opened it immediately:

There would be only one condition, that the men and officers surrendered shall be disqualified from taking up arms again against the government of the United States until properly exchanged.

I was surprised at the generous terms he offered as I knew by previous experience that General Grant usually asked for unconditional surrender. I handed the note to Major Venable and asked, “How would you answer this?”

He said angrily, “I would answer no such letter!”

“Ah,” I said, “but it must be answered.”

And answer it I would, for that afternoon General Custer captured all our supplies at Appomattox Station along with four railroad cars full of food.

That night we could see the Federal campfires ahead and to the west, there was Sheridan, chafing at the bit like an ill-omened bird of prey.

With this in mind, I called a council of my officers.[93] To my great surprise they echoed Longstreet saying to a man, "Not Yet."

All day, April 8th Grant tried to keep up with his troops chasing me. What he got for his trouble was a massive headache. That night he lay down to sleep and was awakened at midnight with my answer. It was colored by my successes that day fighting off his following troops.

I wrote:

I do not propose the surrender of the Army of Northern Virginia. To be frank I do not think the emergency has risen to call for the surrender of this army. But I would like to meet with you at 10 in the morning, not to negotiate a surrender but merely to see how your proposal may affect the Confederate States forces under my command and tend to the restoration of peace.

---

[93] Gordon wrote later: Lee's dignity was amazing. We knew by our own aching hearts that his was breaking, yet he commanded himself and stood calmly facing and discussing the long-dreaded inevitable."

When Grant lay down again and tried to sleep, Rawlins heard him mutter, "It looks like Lee intends to fight."

But Sheridan had my supplies and he also was directly in front of me. I knew I could brush him aside. But if he had infantry… then I knew I would have to surrender and I would have rather died a thousand deaths.

****

The next morning at daybreak General Gordon saw Sheridan and his horsemen at his front. With no reservation he charged at Sheridan, yelling to Major Grimes to, "Clear the road of Yankees." Grimes charged but instead of meeting the charge Sheridan's men backed up and then parted leaving a great gap that the Rebels quickly moved through.

The joyful Rebels crested a ridge that had just been vacated by the Federal Cavalry and stopped. What they saw at their front was masses of men in blue that stretched for miles, and the mass of men were in rows that were as wide as most of the rivers in the south. The Federal infantry had arrived.

Unbeknown to me, at 4 a.m. Sheridan's Infantry had arrived. The Yankees had won the race.

With this turn of events I knew we were done, but I asked Gordon for a report anyway.

He replied:

General, I have fought my corps to a frazzle, and I fear I can do nothing unless I am heavily supported by Longstreet's corps.

Of course Longstreet could support no one.

After reading the message I thought for a moment and then said, "Then there is nothing left me but to go and see General Grant, and I had rather die a thousand deaths."

While waiting for word from Grant about our 10 o'clock meeting I asked my commanders to meet with me. When they came, I first said, "We are surrounded, the men are weak and exhausted and our ammunition is low. I have had a note from General Grant agreeing to meet me on April 9th. Now I ask you all, should we surrender?"

This time Longstreet said, "Your situation speaks for itself."

Mahone agreed with him, but then Porter Alexander surprised me by saying, "If we surrender, all the other armies will follow suit like a row of falling bricks. This army should slip away and continue the fight."

I shook my head and calmly but firmly said to Alexander, "If I took your advice, the men would be without food and have no officer to guide them. Thus they would be forced to rob and steal, becoming nothing less than marauders. Then the enemy would pursue them all over the South, going into areas they would not ordinarily go. It would take years for our country to recover."

Alexander had not a single word in reply. Finally he said, "Sir, you have answered my suggestion from a plane far above me. I am ashamed of having made the proposal."

At half past eight, I mounted Traveller along with Colonels Marshall and Taylor. Taylor motioned to Sergeant Tucker and he joined our sad caravan. We had no white flag of surrender, but the Federals to the right and left of us just gaped. Feeling uncomfortable in the situation, I was glad to see Colonel

Whittier dashing through the lines with a message in his hand. As I hoped it was from Grant. When I read the note my heart fell.

APRIL 9, 1865
General R. E. Lee:
Your note of yesterday is received. As I have no authority to treat on the subject of peace; the meeting proposed for 10 a.m. to-day could lead to no good. I will state, however, General, that I am equally anxious for peace with you, and the whole North entertains the same feeling. The terms upon which peace can be had are well understood. By the South laying down their arms they will hasten that most desirable event, save thousands of human lives, and hundreds of millions of property not yet destroyed. Seriously hoping that all our difficulties may be satisfied without the loss of another life, I subscribe myself, &c., *U.S. Grant,*

Lieutenant-General.

His note left me no room for negotiations. With a heavy heart I asked Taylor to compose the following note:

HEADQUARTERS ARMY OF NORTHERN VIRGINIA,
APRIL 9, 1865
Lieut. Gen. U.S. Grant:
I received your note of this morning on the picket line, whither I had come to meet you and ascertain definitely what terms were embraced in your proposal of yesterday with reference to the surrender of this army. I now ask for an interview in accordance with the offer contained in your letter of yesterday for that purpose.
R. E. Lee, General

There were tears in my eyes when I finished the message. I wanted Grant to call a truce and meet me right where I was but a Federal soldier came dashing through the line, his horse lathered and breathing hard. He pulled up short in front of me and said, "Sir, These Federal skirmishers you see in front of you are leading an attack. You must go back to your lines."

Ignoring the warning, I had Taylor write a new note devoid of any pretense of negotiation. It was a request for a truce awaiting the adjustment of the terms of the surrender of my army.

Then noticing the skirmishers advancing almost on top of us, and wanting to avoid an incident that would interfere with the surrender, I reluctantly rode back to my lines. When I got there, I wrote a note to General Gordon asking him to arrange a truce. He did so, but during the lull that followed Gordon got a surprise, a visitor named Custer.

Custer rode up brandishing his sword and exclaimed, "General Sheridan sends his compliments and demands the surrender of all your troops."

Gordon, flushed with anger, abruptly rejected the demand.

Undeterred, Custer then demanded to see General Longstreet.

Laughing to himself and hoping to stay around when Longstreet dealt with this rude interloper, Gordon swiftly made arrangements for the two of them to meet. It turned out to be more explosive than any other battle that day.

It is safe to say that on this day of heart-breaking surrender Longstreet was in no mood to suffer a fool. And a fool Custer was.

Custer stormed up to Longstreet and blurted out, “In the name of General Sheridan, I demand the unconditional surrender of this army.”

Longstreet blew up like the crater at Petersburg. As he spoke, every voice in the army was stilled except his and the ground fairly shook with his reply to Custer.

“First of all, you damned idiot, I am not the commander of this army. Secondly you are within my lines without authority. And last, you are addressing a superior officer and in disrespect to General Grant as well as myself.”

An obviously shaken Custer then said, “Well then, you and you alone will be responsible for the bloodshed to follow.”

In a gesture of dismissal Longstreet turned his back to the brash general and said in an ominously quiet voice, "Go ahead, and we'll give you all the bloodshed you want."

Thus admonished, Custer sheepishly withdrew, and with head down rode back to his lines.

During the tirade by Longstreet, Meade had called a truce. Then a strange event occurred. The generals from both sides wandered into the space between the two armies and began to fraternize. It was as if they were on a Sunday lark. They greeted each other cordially and mingled together and chatted. Meanwhile my exhaustion caught up with me and I sat down under a tree.

At 11:a.m., Grant, also exhausted and nursing a sick headache, stopped to rest. He had just sat down when a horseman on a mount that was frothing at the mouth, rode up. The man leaped off before the horse stopped and raced over to General Grant. "Ssssir," the courier stuttered, it's a letter from General Lee, Sir."

Grant read the note stoically then handed it to his chief-of-staff to read it aloud. He started to read it and then stopped suddenly. "General Grant, this note is a request to discuss the surrender of his army."

Grant smiled and said, "My headache is gone."

Grant immediately wrote a note back to Lee saying:

I will push forward to the front for the purpose of meeting with you.

Grant

When the courier brought the note back to me, I stood and read it.

As I mounted Traveller, Longstreet said quietly, "Unless he offers us honorable terms, come back and let us fight it out."

I smiled and then turned to Colonel Marshall. "Go find us a suitable meeting place, Charles."

Marshall's face showed he was surprised at my informality. I had never before used his first name.

Marshall spurred his horse ahead of me to Appomattox Station. In a strange coincidence, he met up with Wilmer McLean.

Four years ago Mr. McLean had a farm at Manassas. The first major battle of the war had been fought on his land. In fact his kitchen had even been bombarded during the battle. That was enough for him and after the battle he moved away, he thought, from future war-like events. But here it was again as both armies were descending upon him once again.

After showing Marshall a vacant house that Marshall refused, McLean suggested his own residence. When he saw the house Marshall pronounced it as "perfect for a meeting."

Marshall sent word back to me and I arrived at the McLean house at 1 p.m. I sat down at a marble topped table and waited for Grant. I rarely showed impatience, but as Marshall noted, I was apparently tapping my fingers on the tabletop.

A half hour later, Grant showed up and I stood up.

"The two commanders could have not appeared more different," Marshall later said. "Lee was tall, and dignified with a white beard and immaculate uniform. His dress sword scraped the ground when he sat down.

Grant carried no sword and his uniform was mud splattered and wrinkled. He slouched a bit and his hair was brown and his beard red.

Before Grant sat down, he beckoned to some Federal officers and they entered the room. One of them was Robert Todd Lincoln, the President's son."

Instead of gloating or rejoicing, Grant thought, I felt sad and depressed at the downfall of a foe, who had fought so long and so gallantly. Also I felt badly at the way my uniform looked as Lee might think it showed me discourteous to him.

Grant and I talked about horses and Mexico for a while until I reminded him why we were there. "I suppose, General Grant, that the purpose of our meeting is fully understood. I asked to see you to ascertain upon what terms you would receive the surrender of my army."

Grant smiled and repeated the original, generous offer. "That is, the officers and men surrendered to be paroled and disqualified from taking up arms again until properly exchanged, and all arms, ammunition and supplies to be delivered up as captured property."

I listened carefully and then, after waiting a few moments said, "Why don't you or one of your aides write out the terms so they can formally be acted upon."

Grant gestured to one of his aides, an Indian named Lieutenant Colonel Ely Parker, to bring him his order book.

He then lit a cigar and took the book from his aide. He then paused for a while smoking and thinking. Suddenly his eyes sparkled and he began writing. After a while he paused again and tapped the pencil on the book. Then he began to write once more. After a few minutes, he stopped and handed the book to Parker and sat back contented.

Parker pointed a few things out to Grant and they quickly made some changes. When they were finished Grant handed the book to me.

I was anything but calm as I accepted the book. I noticed my hand was moist and shaking a bit, so I put the book down on the table and took off my glasses. For the next minute or so, I polished the lenses with my handkerchief until I calmed down completely. And then, still a bit fidgety, I picked up the book and stared out the window for a few moments. Finally, with a resigned sigh, I pulled out my handkerchief and wiped both lenses of my glasses. Then I put one steel wire of the glasses behind my right ear and the other wire behind my left, then I began to read.

In accordance with the substance of my letter to you of the 8th instant, I propose to receive the surrender of the Army of Northern Virginia on the following terms, to wit:

Rolls of all the officers and men to be made in duplicate, one copy to be given to an officer designated by me, the other to be retained by such officer or officers as you may designate; the officers to give their individual paroles not to take up arms against the Government of the United States until properly exchanged, and each company or regimental commander to sign a like parole for the men of his command.

The arms, artillery and public property are to be parked and stacked, and turned over to the officer appointed by me to receive them. This will not embrace the sidearms of the officers, nor their private horses or baggage. This done, officers and men will be allowed to return to their homes, not to be disturbed by United States authority so long as they observe their paroles and the laws in force where they may reside.

I read the epistle twice to make sure I understood it. I knew when I finished and put the book down that General Grant's terms would have a very happy effect on the men of my army.

I looked at Grant, handed him the book and said, "This is most generous, General Grant. The men of my army will be very grateful to you."

Then I hesitated and drummed my fingers on the table.

Grant smiled and said, "Is there something else you wish to say, General Lee?"

"Yes. There is one more thing. The enlisted men in our cavalry and artillery own their own horses. Will the men be permitted to take these horses with them?"

Grant thought a moment and then said, "The terms we set down do not permit this… But the subject is new to me…" He paused for a few moments and then said, "I assume that most of the men in your army are small farmers and that they will need to put in a crop for their families before the next winter. Of course this would be difficult to do without the horses they are now riding. I will instruct the officers I appoint to let all those men who claim a horse or mule to take their animals home with them."

"This will have the best possible effect on the men and do much toward conciliating our people."

Grant stood up and asked Colonel Bowers to copy the order in ink. The colonel was so nervous he twice dropped the pen. Laughing, General Grant clapped him on the shoulder and handed the pen to Colonel Parker.

While Parker was writing I told Colonel Marshall to write the formal Confederate acceptance.

While they were writing I mentioned to General Grant that we had about a thousand Federal prisoners and were unable to feed them. "Indeed," I said "we have nothing for my own men."

Grant immediately ordered the captured men to be fed and released. Then he laughed good-naturedly. "And feed the Confederates while you're at it."

At three o'clock everything was ready and with great reluctance I signed the terms of surrender and acceptance. Grant quickly signed after me.

When the signing was done, I saw no reason to stay any longer and stood. Grant rose with me and took my hand. After his most generous terms to a helpless enemy, I held no animosity toward him and shook his hand warmly.

I then turned and thanking the sergeant that held the door open, walked out on the porch. To my surprise all the Federal soldiers in the Mclean yard snapped to attention and saluted smartly. I smiled and returned the salute. I stepped down two steps and paused. Then I stared toward where my army was pondering whether they would have to fight again.

Absently I struck the palm of my left hand with my right fist three times, then my voice cracking a bit, I called to Sergeant Tucker to bring my horse, Traveller, to me. When the horse approached me, I patted him fondly – my old warhorse – and put my left foot in the stirrup. I leaned against Traveller almost devoid of strength. Then realizing where I was, I began to mount the horse. As I did, the pain I felt in my heart was so strong, I groaned as I put my right leg over the saddle.

General Grant then took off his hat in salute. And all the other Federals followed suit. I nodded my head and then took off my own hat to answer their honor, and slowly rode toward my men.

When I got to my lines, the men crowded around me. A sergeant tried to get them to back off, but I gestured him away.

The men about me spoke. “Are we surrendered, Gen’ral?” “We kin still whup ‘em Gen’ral!” “You get to the rear, Gen’ral and we’ll get y’all ter General Johnston.”

At that last statement my control left me and tears flowed down my cheeks, my grief showing for all to see. The men quickly quieted down.

My voice trembling I spoke through my tears. “Men, we have fought through the war together. I have done the best I could for you. My heart is too full for me to say more."

I then went to my headquarters tent, asked everyone there to leave and spent the next hour grieving for my army, my state and my way of life.

I began to pace the floor and made any visitor know that I wanted no company. Meanwhile, I endured the shouting and celebration of the Yankees at their victory. Finally they quieted. I later heard Grant stopped them, and I was left alone with my thoughts.

I realized I couldn't leave my men without an official goodbye so I sat down at my desk and started writing:

General Order Number 9

After four years of arduous service, marked by unsurpassed courage and fortitude, the Army of Northern Virginia has been compelled to yield to overwhelming numbers and resources.

I need not tell the brave survivors of so

many hard fought battles, who have remained steadfast to the last, that I have consented to this result from no distrust of them.

But feeling that valor and devotion could accomplish nothing that could compensate for the loss that must have attended the continuance of the contest, I determined to avoid the useless sacrifice of those whose past services have endeared them to their countrymen

By the terms of the agreement officers and men can return to their homes and remain until exchanged. You will take with you the satisfaction that proceeds from the consciousness of duty faithfully performed and I earnestly pray that a Merciful God will extend to you his blessing and protection.

With an increasing admiration of your constancy and devotion to your country, and a grateful remembrance *of your kind and generous consideration for myself, I bid you an affectionate farewell.*

R.E. Lee

****

I had thought Grant would let us go home, but on that one item he was firm. There was to be a formal surrender of the Confederate troops with a giving up of weapons and flags.

The morning of April 12th came as gray and cold as my heart. Although Grant had gone to report to Lincoln in Washington, I had not left as I wished to be there when my men started home. Although I was not a witness to the surrender, I will let General Gordon's report to me tell the reader what occurred:

I woke on April 12th and forgetting my multiple wounds tried to rise up quickly out of my cot. Reality soon caught up with me and, first falling back, got up slowly and carefully.

On this date that will live in history I was asked by General Lee to surrender the Army of Northern Virginia to General Grant's Army of the Potomac.

It would be gratifying to me, and in accordance with my sense of justice to mention the acts of individual courage displayed by the men of this army, both by my own observation and what has been reported to me. But as the display of this virtue of heroism was the general rule, I should do an injustice to too many others if I attempted it.

But wait a moment. Why should I tell you about my brave lads surrendering when my learned friend Joshua Chamberlain told about them and my part in it, and told it so beautifully.

John B. Gordon

There is nothing left for me but go and see General Grant and I would rather die a thousand deaths.

General Robert E. Lee

Chapter 42: The Surrender

The daybreak was cold and gray, depressing to the senses. But my heart was filled with warmth. I had suffered many wounds in the war and the weather of the early morning added to my discomfort as I rose out of my cot. But as I had done so many times before I ignored the pain.

Today is a special day and I dressed in my finest uniform. Then I left my tent and proceeded to the principle street that ran through Appomattox where the surrender would take place. It was supposed to be an honor for me but just now, limping and shivering in the gray dawn the honor escaped me.

When I got to the street in question no one was in sight so I dismounted and looked around me. The sky was dark and I said a small prayer hoping that it wouldn't rain.

Slowly, as if in a dream the Federal army began to appear and formed on both sides of the street. They stood there at ease talking quietly. I didn't interfere with their relaxed state. They had enough of martinet officers.

Suddenly a sergeants deep bass voice crying out, "Army of the Potomac, Attttttttenshun!"

Both lines quickly came to attention getting ready to receive the last remnants of the men, colors and armaments of that great army which ours had been created to confront.

In the distance I could see the Confederate troops gathering together to cross a valley and come to us. They first took down their shelter tents and folded them carefully as if they were precious things, then they slowly formed ranks morosely as they would have for an unwelcome duty.

When they reached the street there were no bands, no drums just the familiar shuffling sound of marching feet. Just then the sun broke through the clouds and glinted off their muskets carried at right shoulder shift.

On they came with the old swinging route step and swaying battle flags led by General John B. Gordon on his horse, and followed up by the old Stonewall brigade, now reduced to a bare 200 men.

What greeting shall we give this pageant of men that has already been spoken in volleys of muskets on the banks of the Potomac, the James and the Mississippi? There is none, no greeting ever made that can match their valor.

Gordon sat erect on his horse, named *Milroy*, his expression dark. The men behind him, although they kept their lines well dressed and their formation tight under the scrutiny of their former enemies, were equally grim. Before us, humiliated but proud, came the men whom neither toil, suffering, nor disaster, nor death could shake them from their resolve. They came before us now thin, worn, famished but erect, eyes looking level into ours, waking memories that will bind us through eternity. Was not such manhood to be welcomed back into the Union?

As the column neared the double line of Federal soldiers Gordon responded to a spoken order, a bugle call and an electrifying sound; the clatter of hundreds of FEDERAL muskets being raised to the shoulder. Gordon's head snapped up. He wheeled his mount toward me and made Milroy and himself one uplifted figure. The animal reared then dipped its head toward the ground. At that moment, Gordon raised his sword aloft and brought its tip down to his toe in a sweeping response to the Federal tribute. When the horses front legs landed General Gordon shouted a command and the advancing Confederates came from a right shoulder shift to shoulder arms returning the Federal salute. It was honor, answering honor, and so touching a moment many of the grizzled veterans wept. The Confederates then reached the end of the street and began to stack their arms and cartridges.

Lastly, and reluctantly, with agony written on every one of their faces, they carefully fold their flags, battle-worn and torn, blood stained with heart holding colors, and tearfully lay them down.

After a short while they formed up again and in silence left the field.

As they walked away on our part there was not a sound of trumpet, nor roll of drum; and not a cheer, but an awed stillness and breath-holding as if it were the passing of the dead.

The end

Epilogue

The day after the surrender the men of the Army of Northern Virginia left for their homes. Robert E. Lee was among them since the Federals had taken his home at Arlington for a cemetery. He left for his new home his family had made in Richmond.

Before he left Appomattox for Richmond, the Federal cavalry insisted on riding with him, at least part way, as an honor guard. Lee objected, but they insisted.

After Lee's surrender at Appomattox, President Lincoln pardoned him.

When he got to Richmond, he promptly moved his family to Lexington Virginia. He was then offered many different jobs, mostly for his name, such as bank president, life insurance executive and, a job that several other generals did take, a state lottery administrator. He rejected all of them.

Then came an offer to be president of Washington College in Lexington, Virginia.

Although the salary of $1,500 a year was small, Lee said yes to something he could do well and would be meaningful.

In 1865, Lee signed an amnesty oath, asking once again to become a citizen of the United States. He did so, not only as an example but also as an active encouragement for confederate soldiers to rejoin the United States. But General Lee's desire to become a full-fledged American fell victim to an error. His oath of allegiance was lost, and he was a man without a country when he died of heart failure in 1870.

In 1970, 100 years later, a clerk in Washington found the misplaced oath in the National Archives.

On August 5, 1975, at a ceremony at Arlington House, President Gerald Ford called Lee an example to succeeding generations and had his citizenship restored. He is buried on the grounds of the former Washington College, now known as Washington and Lee University.

Edward Aronoff

Dr. Edward Aronoff is the author of several books including the award winning *Betrayal at Gettysburg*, as well as:

Three Came Home Vol. I – Lorena
Three Came Home Vol. II – Sam
Three Came Home Vol. III – Rutherford
Toxic Food/Healthy Food
Last Chance
The Pagliacci Affair

Dr. Aronoff was educated in New York, Iowa and Florida, and began a medical practice in the Tampa Bay area. Moving on to a literary career, he has been writing ever since. He has four children, nine grandchildren, and lives with his wife in Florida and the mountains of North Carolina.